To Dave
from
Eleanor

March, 1939

THE AMERICAN THEATRE

Norman Bel Geddes: *The Divine Comedy*

THE
AMERICAN
THEATRE

By JOHN ANDERSON

AND

THE MOTION PICTURE
IN AMERICA

By RENE FÜLÖP-MILLER

THE DIAL PRESS·NEW YORK·1938

PRINTED IN THE UNITED STATES OF AMERICA

Van Rees Press · New York

FOR MARGOT

CONTENTS

THE AMERICAN THEATRE

THE MOTION PICTURE IN AMERICA

THE AMERICAN THEATRE

AN INTERPRETIVE HISTORY

By

JOHN ANDERSON

There are, as anyone may discover by glancing at the library shelves, many books on the American theatre, ranging from brief critical studies of individuals, to Professor Odell's ten-volume history of the New York Stage. There are biographies and autobiographies of actors, managers, and playwrights, and there are bales of newspaper and magazine articles to supplement these larger works.

If I may anticipate the obvious question, then, I may define the intentions of the present volume, and, by setting its limits, excuse (or at least explain) its omissions. For its scope is by no means all inclusive. It is strictly a sketch of the American theatre in its relation to the drama, and in its later portions an examination of the theatre through the work of the men writing plays for it.

By confining this study to the playhouses and the artists who animate them, I am aware that much colorful material is neglected. The work of the theatre's frontiersmen makes a fascinating record, but in its wealth of detail and its duplication, it is bound to lie outside the narrow boundaries set for the study of main channels.

Nor is it exactly within the present purpose to explore the festive regions occupied by burlesque, minstrels, vaudeville, musical comedies, and that exuberantly American manifestation of the stage—the revue. No one would deny for a moment that they are important aspects of the theatre, and I omit them, reluctantly, only to maintain the direct line of the discussion and to keep the central theme steadily in focus.

Within these limits I have attempted merely to sketch, as concisely as possible, the chief historical events, and to subject them, with some attempted perspective, to a critical appraisal. This is, therefore, an interpretative history, and its application for shelf-room will be, I hope, considered on that inflection in the belief that a theatre with such a past deserves a future.

JOHN ANDERSON.

Green Rising,
Stepney Depot, 1938.

COLONIAL BIRTH PAINS

CHAPTER I

COLONIAL BIRTH PAINS

IN DISCUSSIONS OF THE AMERICAN THEATRE the point is frequently made that there is no such thing—what we have is merely a transplanted European theatre. Courteous, but misguided historians have, it is true, tried to saddle us with strange Indian derivations, and in support of this notion they have pretended to discover in O'Neill's use of masks, and a midsummer liking for pageants and opera al fresco, a survival of the aboriginal folk ways in modern times. This is simply a fresh aspect of the old European suspicion that all Americans secretly

first theatrical performance in the Western Hemisphere took place in Williamsburg, Virginia, in New York, or, as Odell with stinging precision points out, in Mexico during the first decade after the conquest.

For the benefit of those who cherish such information the first definite record of a theatrical performance in the American Colonies is, unhappily, a police record. In 1665, some venturesome citizens in the settlement of Accomac, in Virginia, put on a playlet called *Ye Bare and Ye Cubb* on August 27 of that year, and were forthwith ordered to appear in court "in those habiliments that they then acted in, and give a draught of such verses and other speeches which were then acted by them." The defendants were found not guilty, but whether because their performance beguiled the honorable court, or whether the judge indulged in a form of higher criticism and decided it was not a performance and not a play, we know not.

The incident is useful only in showing an early attitude towards the theatre, because the attitude still appears now and then to startle the theatre with the threat of censorship and similar attempts at witch-burnings.

In 1684 Boston was in a Puritanical fever over what the "Ministers of Christ at Boston" called "Gynecandrical dancing," and in 1686 and 1687 the town was upset by "cock-skailing" and stage fights.

The first record of a licensed performance shows that the Governor of New York received and approved somewhere between 1699 and 1702 a petition by one Richard Hunter who, with considerable optimism "had been at great charge and expense in providing persons and necessary's in order to the acting of plays in this city." Though the license was granted there is no record of a performance and Professor Odell suggests that since the population of the town (according to I. N. Phelps Stokes) was then less than 5,000, Mr. Hunter must have decided not to avail himself of the permit. On the other hand he must have known what his chances of profit were before he "had been at great charge and expense." Mr. Hornblow's history says the population then was 30,000, but Mr. Phelps Stokes found an old census.

We have, at least, Anthony Aston's own statement that when he arrived in Charles-Town "full of Lice, Shame, Poverty, Nakedness, and Hunger" he "turned player and poet" and "wrote one play on the subject of the country." Aston was one of the bright adventurers, who had acted in Drury Lane in his time, and the archaeologists, from internal evidence of Tony Aston's travels, have set the date of his performance as 1703, and a year or so later, from Aston's own records, he played in New York. By 1709 New York had enacted a law forbidding "play acting and prize-fighting," and it is only reasonable to suppose that there must have been some to forbid.

The first play printed in America was a political satire *Androborus* (*The Man-Eater*) and it carries the imprint of William Bradford, 1714 "Monoropolis," which means presumably, "Fools-Town." The Henry E. Huntington library contains the only known copy of this play, and Mr. Phelps Stokes thinks it was acted by and for the governor's household.

It was a ferocious attack upon the administration of Trinity Parish, and its authorship, since the name "Hunter" is written on the title page, is attributed to the then Governor, Robert Hunter, who was a friend of Addison and Steele. Various authorities, especially Paul Leicester Ford, believe that it was never performed because, as Mr. Ford puts it, "the plot turns on so filthy an incident as to preclude its performance even in the coarse and vulgar time of its writing."

Mr. Hornblow, who seems to have examined the background of this play more thoroughly than other historians, not only attributes its authorship to Governor Hunter but says that he wrote it in collaboration with Lewis Morris, "a native New Yorker and chief justice of the New York Colony." Since Mr. Hornblow traced the single surviving copy through the ownership of Garrick, Kemble, and the Duke of Devonshire it may be supposed that he is fully documented, though his sources are not clear.

Two or three more dates of minor events will bring us quickly to the real beginnings of the theatre in colonial America. It is of passing interest to note that while the Governor of New York was writing a play too indecent to perform, law or no law, Boston was taking firm measures against the drama. (Justice) Samuel Sewall records in his diary a letter written to the Governor and Council. There had been a rumor that a play would be acted in the Council Chamber and Mr. Sewall announced "as much as in me lyes I do forbid it." The Town House he suggested was not to be abused with "dances or other scenical divertisements."

The other incident is the famous and somehow still hilarious attempt of Governor Spottiswood of Virginia to give a public entertainment in 1718 in honor of His Majesty's birthday. As a generous gesture all gentlemen that would come would be admitted to the play ordered for the occasion. By some mischievous instinct not one member of the House of Assembly would pay the Governor "the common compliment of a visit," but got up a big party of their own, had a roaring time of it and took no more notice of the Governor "than if there had been none in the place." The historical point of this incident, if any, lies in the fact that the Governor did have a company of actors and there is a contract dated July 11, 1716 and recorded at Yorktown between William Levinstone and Charles and Mary Stagg. Mr. Levinstone, a merchant of the town, should be celebrated in any proper history as the forerunner of a long line of patrons of the drama, spiritual ancestor of the "angel" as the modern theatre has come to know this valuable, stage-struck and occasionally demented breed. It had been Mr. Levinstone's pleasure to manage a dancing school in New Kent County and the chief dancers in this school were Mr. and Mrs. Stagg. Within a few months Mr. Levinstone had lived up to his contract and we find the theatre mentioned in *The Present State of Virginia* by Hugh Jones, published in London, in 1724 as *The Playhouse and Good Bowling Green*.

Since the few newspapers extant at that time contained almost no reference to the theatre, chronology becomes difficult. One line in an advertisement in the New York *Gazette* in October, 1733, presents the only evidence that New York had a theatre. It is an advertisement for the sale of miscellaneous items including "a negro girl about sixteen years of age, has had the smallpox and is fit for town or country." Inquirers were urged to see Mr. George Talbot and the notice added for our information "next door to the Play House." It was in this theatre, presumably, that "the ingenious Mr. Thomas Heady," barber and perruque-maker to His Honor, acted *The Recruiting Officer*. Whatever its merits, this performance antedates by twenty years the arrival of the Hallams in Virginia and the beginnings of a formal history of the theatre in America.

As to the nature of these early performances, the authorities, from the beginning, have indulged in occasionally heated controversies. Dunlap, in his vivid but often inaccurate record of the early American theatre, written from what must have been a slightly tottering memory, seems to think that most of them were amateur and not very good. Seilhamer, probably for no better reason than to contradict poor Dunlap, thinks better of them. Doubtless, many of the performances were put on by small groups, possibly with a professional actor as the nucleus.

It is certain, however, that by the time that the Hallams arrived the colonial theatre was becoming a faint carbon copy of its London model. Dunlap refers to public complaints against the number of gentlemen crowded on the stage during the performance, and a novel dealing with the Williamsburg period contains a conversational aside between a player and a gallant.

With the Hallams we come to companies of professional actors. As a background for this emigration of English actors to the Colonies, it may be pointed out that from the first settlement in Virginia actors had been forbidden. The Elizabethan stage was overcrowded and this ban against players caused deep discontent in London, where the theatre promptly exacted reprisals by making fun of the settlements of the New World. With the arrival of the Hallams the Atlantic became the one-way theatrical thoroughfare it remains to this day.

The Hallam Company was the property of William Hallam, who was the proprietor of one of the smaller non-patent London theatres. When he was driven to the wall by London competition he assembled a company of fifteen players, a few costumes, some scenery, properties and so on, put the whole business in charge of his brother, Lewis, and so launched the first important theatrical venture in America. For two years the Hallam Company played in various colonial towns, mostly in Shakespearian and Restoration dramas, beginning in Williamsburg with the *Merchant of Venice*. Two years later the venture came to a premature conclusion when Hallam took his company to the West Indies and there, quite forlornly, died. The company disbanded. It is convenient to cling to the Hallams' appearance in Williamsburg as the first professional company in a building erected as a theatre, but it would be inaccurate to imply that other theatres lacked professional performances. The Hallams, as a matter of fact, had played in New York, but the so-called New Theatre was merely a large room in the upper part of a building near the junction of Pearl

Street and Maiden Lane. This auditorium had a platform stage and raised seats and was capable of seating about four hundred persons.

There is some doubt as to whether the New Theatre and the so-called First Nassau Street Theatre were separate buildings. T. Allston Brown, in *A History of the New York Stage* describes the Nassau Street Theatre in detail, indicating that Judge Daly in his book *First Theatre in America* is wrong in assuming that the New and the First Nassau Street were one and the same.

As an interesting picture of a theatre of that time Mr. Brown's description is worth reprinting: "It was a two-storied house with high gables. The stage was raised five feet from the floor. The scenes, curtains and wings were all carried by the managers in their 'property' trunks. A green curtain was suspended from the ceiling. A pair of paper screens were erected upon the right and left hand sides for wings. Six wax lights were in front of the stage. The orchestra consisted of a German flute, horn and drum players. Suspended from the ceiling was the chandelier, made of a barrel hoop, through which were driven half a dozen nails into which were stuck so many candles. Two drop scenes representing a castle and a wood, bits of landscape, river and mountain comprised the scenery."

In the unsettled condition of the early theatre no one would risk heavy investments in the physical well-being of an institution that was under steady attack. Local prejudice against the theatre was such that in Philadelphia a hospital refused to accept the money raised by a benefit performance, and in New-port, Rhode Island, when Douglass appeared with the first professional company to play in New England, he avoided opposition by billing *Othello* as *A Series of Moral Dialogues, in Five Parts, Depicting the Evils of Jealousy and other Bad Passions, and Proving that Happiness can only Spring from the Pursuit of Virtue.* To placate public opinion he resorted to the old trick of calling his house "A Histrionic Academy," a term much used in England, even by such players as Mrs. Siddons and John Philip Kemble. Pennsylvania enacted a law providing a penalty of five hundred pounds for anyone who built a theatre or sold tickets for a theatrical entertainment. The law was set aside by the King's Council.

It is small wonder, therefore, that the theatre buildings were rough, barnlike structures, usually painted red, lighted by candles or oil lamps, and virtually unheated. Where candles were used they were so placed that spectators could trim them, if inclined, and it was customary, in love scenes, or scenes of tragedy, for someone to step on the stage and snuff out some of the lights to give the ensuing incidents the required shading.

Though the theatre was entirely English in its plays and players, its social customs did reflect something of the surrounding society. It was patronized, as usual, by the upper and lower social strata and took on attributes of its supporters. Both elements were doubtless represented by one of the early signs concerning the heating arrangements. Ladies and gentlemen were requested to bring their own foot warmers, and all

15

members of the audience were "respectfully requested not to spit on the stove."

Two advertisements printed around the middle of the century suggest something of the audiences. The first, part of Hallam's announcement, reads:

"Ladies engaging seats in the boxes are advised to send their servants early on the day of the performance to hold them and prevent trouble and disappointment."

The other, less than a decade later, was inserted by Douglass:

"A Pistole reward will be given to whoever can discover the person who was so very rude as to throw Eggs from the Gallery upon the Stage last Monday, by which the Cloaths of some Ladies and Gentlemen were spoiled, and the performance, in some measure, interrupted."

A Pistole, it may be noted, was a Spanish coin, valued at about $3.80, in circulation in the Colonies at that time. Mr. Douglass's conservatism in estimating an interruption, is not so easily evaluated.

One further note will indicate that the theatre's problems have always been much the same:

"To prevent accidents by carriages meeting," said the announcement of the opening of the John Street Theatre in New York, "it is requested that those coming to the House may enter John Street from the Broad Way, and returning, drive from thence down John street, into Nassau street, or forward to that known by the name of Cart and Horse street, as may be most convenient."

This last event marks a period in which, despite the steady opposition, the theatre made great advances.

As the Revolution approached the theatre began its first movement away from England's apron strings, but still failed to reflect, in the seething political events, anything of the Revolutionary temper, except in such isolated "dialogues" as *The Rising Glory of America*.

With a timidity towards politics which has persisted into later years the colonial theatre cast merely a pale reflection of the times. Its audiences were still given the usual classics in the repertory companies, and though there is very little evidence of current affairs on the stage, some external events had significance.

The Stamp Act in 1765 caused the first open demonstration against the English players, and resulted in the partial destruction, by a mob, of the Beekman Street Theatre. Douglass's company was away during the riot, and the theatre was fixed up in time for the actors to give performances a few weeks later, but the name of the group was naïvely changed from "The Company of Comedians From London" to "The American Company." Nevertheless its advertisement for *The Prince of Parthia* at the Southwark theatre, Philadelphia, two years later ended the public notice with "Vivant Rex et Regina."

In a country moving swiftly toward an outbreak of war with England the theatre provided few events of historical importance. Thinking possibly to take advantage of the rising feeling against England a few members of Douglass's company formed "The Virginia Company of Comedians" but it was a

17

short-lived venture. This period is chiefly notable for the first appearance of a native-born actor on the American stage. This honor is somewhat doubtfully divided between a Mr. Goodman who appeared in Douglass's company during one of its visits to Philadelphia and John E. Martin, a New Yorker. Both were young lawyers with a leaning towards the theatre. Goodman appeared in 1769 and Martin in 1790. The difficulty is that some historians claim that Mr. Goodman was born in London.

By October 1774 Congress, meeting in Philadelphia, passed a resolution requesting the suspension of all public amusements. The suspension was not made compulsory until four years later, but in 1776 a group of British officers in Boston so far ignored the matter as to present a piece generally credited to General Burgoyne and called, *The Blockade of Boston*. The incident holds some historical glamour, because during the presentation of the play on January 8, in Faneuil Hall, a British sergeant interrupted the performance by shouting, "The Yankees are attacking our works on Bunker's Hill." The audience thought this was part of the fun until General Howe shouted "Officers, to your alarm posts." According to Timothy Newell's diary there was "much fainting, fright and confusion." Another diarist says that the performance was given fourteen days later.

This minor incident is notable chiefly as the target of one of the first satirical plays written by an American. The author was Mrs. Mercy Warren, wife of General Warren, who made fun of the incident in a play with the punning title, *The Blockhead, Or the Affrighted Officers.*

With the suppression of the theatre most of the professional players took themselves off to the West Indies and left the playhouses entirely to the British soldiers; it was during this period curiously enough that the native dramatists began to emerge. Until this time, the theatrical fare, as we have seen, was exclusively English and since no American royalties were paid on a seemingly inexhaustible supply the managers had no interest in native material. A few pamphleteers emerged and tried to use the theatre as the vehicle for their opinions but without much success. But by 1782 the military players were dispersing. In the post-Revolutionary confusion, the theatre went again into eclipse and while the professional players began to drift back the general feeling was that the public was not ready.

In spite of the war-time laws against the theatre, the year 1787 brings us to the first play by an American author on an American theme to be produced on the American stage. Royall Tyler's *The Contrast* had far-reaching effects, though it is doubtful, as some historians contend, that it changed the public attitude. In an art that appeals at once to the snobbish as well as the herd instincts of the public the change may be attributed to the favor of General Washington. The first President was an ardent playgoer, sometimes, in a worshipful audience, to his own embarrassment.

Mr. Tyler's success was truly the success of the amateur. As a Harvard student he had shown some facility in writing, but apparently had no serious inclination in that direction and seemed to lose sight of his talents during the Revolution in which he achieved the rank of Major. On his first visit to New York, he saw a performance of *The School for Scandal* and decided at once to borrow the pattern for an American theme. Without the robustious performances of his time the old play seems a little thin and plotless, but it probably had some go to it, in Mr. Wignell's creation of the drama's original Jonathan. There is still a cranky sort of humor to it that has an unmistakably American flavor. The contrast it made was, of course, between the fashionable world and the plain but inevitably honest American ideal. We may still find an echo of its proud native laughter when Jonathan declares his preference for "Tabitha, her Bible, a cow, and a little peaceable bundling."

More important, however, than its effect upon the public was the effect of *The Contrast* on William Dunlap. In an age that took to fatherhood somewhat promiscuously Dunlap was the father of American drama. Even with his great success, Tyler was no professional playwright and wound up his career on the Supreme Court in Vermont. But Dunlap was the real article, and in the course of an eventful lifetime wrote some sixty-odd plays for the theatre whose first historian he was destined, also, to be.

Dunlap was of Irish descent. His father had come to America with General Wolfe and since it was a family of some means, Master William had been sent back to England to study art with Benjamin West. Somewhat tardily, it would seem at this distance, he discovered that his eyesight had been permanently

20

impaired and after a couple of years in London he returned to New York in time to see Tyler's sensational play rounding out a three-year career. That settled it; from then on Dunlap knew his destiny.

In the presence of such a passionate love for the theatre it would be pleasant to add that Dunlap was a master. Unhappily, such was not the case. His plays are very indifferent and he challenges our interest, as his fairest biographer concedes, "almost wholly as a pioneer." He tried theatre management and went bankrupt. Among other biographies he wrote one of George Frederick Cooke, and it was this work of which Lord Byron wrote "such a book! I believe, since 'drunken Barnaby's journal,' nothing like it has drenched the press. All greenroom and taproom, drams and the drama. Brandy, whiskey, punch and latterly toddy overflow every page. Two things are rather marvellous; first that a man should live so long drunk and next that he should have found a sober biographer."

Somehow in his busy lifetime Dunlap found time for other biographies, for a job as assistant Paymaster General of the New York Militia and as founder with Morse, Peale, Ingham and others of the National Academy of Design. In 1828 when he was sixty-two years old he began his *History of the American Theatre* which was published in 1832, six years before his death. Except for his delightful and almost completely unreliable history, it was poor Dunlap's fate to be an echo of other men. His greatest success in the theatre was as adapter of Kotzebue, and in painting his most successful compositions are considered mere copies of West's. Dunlap studied German in

21

order to translate the Kotzebue plays and Professor Odell calls the end of the century "the reign of Kotzebue." Certainly, it was one of the main channels of Gothic influence.

Dunlap had one moment of joy which all the snarling of Seilhamer cannot dim. That was the performance of *Darby's Return* in the John Street Theatre, with General Washington in the audience. Before that he had played the flute for Washington and painted a portrait of him. The author of the play relates the incident with gratifying detail and gusto in his own history and explains how the General was relieved "from apprehension of further personality." So the "Father of the Drama" heard the Father of His Country indulge "in that which was with him extremely rare—a hearty laugh."

It is necessary at this point to examine the theatre in an aspect which encompassed both its greatest expansion and its deepest downfall—its business. In the period after the Revolution there was a natural movement into the newly settled communities of the West and communities gradually developed their own theatres with resident stock companies.

In time this territory appealed to visiting stars, who, before then, had contented themselves with playing the chief cities on the Atlantic seaboard, and it became the custom for important actors to play with the support of the resident companies. Though an insignificant matter of mere experience, this practice had dangerous implications, and through ensuing circumstances, had a profound effect on the course of the whole theatre in America.

For the touring stars caused a double problem, one artistic

and the other financial. They found themselves frequently at odds with the local talent (there were many and often bitter and hilarious instances of resentment) and the public showed plainly that it preferred the stars to the resident players. This made it possible for the stars to make exorbitant demands, and thus force the managers to retrench by cutting the pay of the local companies.

Presently it became almost impossible for a local company to afford a suitable supporting cast for the visiting stars, and so the stars began carrying at first one or two subordinate players, and finally moving from theatre to theatre with whole companies. The local theatre owners had been obliged to accept a subtle but definite change in status. Where they were once producers and in a sense, theatrical artists, they became, under the new system, merely landlords trying to make a piece of real estate pay. In this inadvertent fashion the American theatre embarked upon its most wayward adventure.

For their own part the stars were also desperate, and we shall presently see what effect their desperation had on the only permanently important part of the theatre—its playwrights. Pressed by a clamorous public, they took the course which the theatre has always taken—given it what it wants.

Various theories have been advanced to explain the ensuing events, but it would seem that the final dissolution of local stock companies and the complete establishment of the touring company headed by a star was purely mechanical. Within a period of twelve years around the middle of the nineteenth century, railroads in the United States were increased by many thousands of miles. More territory became easily available. Speedier transportation made it possible for actors to extend their tours and make even more money. The theatre moved towards its not quite final phase of big business, without ever pausing to think that the methods employed in ordinary merchandise may develop flaws when used in marketing such a perishable commodity as art.

Since the control of the theatre is very seldom in the hands of artists it may be pointed out in extenuation that, as a business, it used at this juncture the approved methods of business expansion. The touring stars worked themselves into a situation from which they emerged only by surrendering their autonomy. In attempting to arrange their tours expeditiously they had to resort to bookings, and at first this was a simple matter.

In those leisurely days, when the theatres in New York were clustered in the neighborhood of Union Square, it was the custom for provincial managers to come to New York, see the shows, and book them for certain dates into the outlying theatres. It was still a man-to-man business.

But obviously it was necessary for the stars to conserve their time, and arrange their tours to eliminate waste wherever possible. This gave rise to the fatal middleman, the booking agency. With his office under his hat this parasite emerged in the theatre and presently, by sheer expediency, came to dominate it.

In his initial phases, which are, in such cocoon cases, so often deceptive, he seemed entirely harmless. On the one hand he saved the provincial managers a trip to New York, and on the other he saved the star companies the onerous details of separate dealings in arranging a tour. He made it possible for a star to select a route and follow it with the least possible backtracking, and he saved the local managers, scattered around the country, all the annoyance of barter and the risk of having his theatre empty.

Here was the crux of the matter. The theatre, as a local institution, became not a theatre so much as an investment in real estate which had to yield its utmost in revenue. The way was open for one of those peaceful but eventful revolutions which the world passes through without ever realizing what is happening. The men who had no interest, either as landlords or artists, quietly but firmly seized control of the theatre. The booking agency became the absolute dictator of amusement in virtually every town in the United States. When the local managers became mere branch executives for a central booking office in New York the Syndicate was supreme. By the most approved methods of Big Business, in an age of industrial feudalism (not to say piracy) the theatre calmly, and for the most selfish reasons, surrendered and obligingly choked itself to death.

Its empire, if I may draw this commercial background to a welcome close, did not collapse without a struggle. Indeed the struggle exhausted it. Presently the Syndicate was challenged by a new group, the Brothers Shubert, who, with scanty financing but great energy, set out to break the strangle hold the Erlanger Syndicate had on the whole theatre. It was slow going, and though the course of the fight was spectacular in its com-

25

mercial aspects, the upshot was disastrous. As the challengers gained ground they built theatres all over the country to compete with the Syndicate. The country was overbuilt, and in the heat of their warfare both sides lost sight of the fact (if either ever cared very much) that they were dealing with an art.

With all those theatres and all those actors running around on the perpetually expanding frontiers of railroad mileage, no one had done anything about the essential product the Big Business gentlemen were so ardently exploiting. No one had increased the output of even passable actors, and no one had done anything about providing the theatre with authors. The thing passed beyond the limits of possible consumption. The outlying theatres, brought up to expect the best, found second-, third-, and nth-rate productions palmed off on them as stopgaps in a business warfare. The provinces were sick and tired of Broadway's gyp methods and were ready to quit when the whole matter passed out of the hands of the combatants.

Two events knocked the American theatre, in a strictly territorial sense, into the dustbin: the advent of the movies and the European war. Where the railroads had once been the medium of the theatre's greatest extension they now proved its most serious obstacle. Rates were up. Shipping actors and scenery became almost prohibitive. Companies that failed were frequently left stranded, and in the face of cheaper competition from the motion pictures the theatre finally was obliged to face all its old sins of exploitation and mismanagement. The actors struck, and in winning the strike they saddled the theatre with fresh bosses—the Unions. Now the actors are organized, the scene shifters, the scene painters, the electricians, the musicians, the ushers, and in the infinite wisdom of the Muses, the dramatists. When all of this high-pressured organization had been perfected it seemed for a moment that it was merely the formal routine of a funeral. At its most drastic moment the theatre, whose far-flung frontiers had once mastered a nation, fell back upon the narrow strip of ground on Manhattan Island bounded by Sixth and Eighth avenues, Fortieth and Fifty-second streets. It was a tiny domain, the shrivelled remnants of a once magnificent kingdom, and if there is any point in telling its tale, except as the memory of some far-off forgotten thing, it is not because "the road" may come back, or because the imperial landlords may re-line their pockets, or even that the fickle public may be coaxed again to the little brass wickets, in a rosy Broadway rainbow, but because, stripped of its cheap commercialism, its popular claptrap, and an insular jingoism, it seems ready now to accept its responsibility and to speak, when it finds the voice of a dramatist, with the authority, the insight, and the brilliance of the most eloquent art.

In the years of our snobbish copying, patriotic pioneering, and blatant commercialism no American playwright arose to speak in the terms of authentic drama. There was, until now, no American play, which, beyond its historical or folk-aspects, had the faintest value as dramatic literature. Some of us, who watch by what seems alternately a cradle and a deathbed, suspect that in its direct distress as a commercial ruin, our theatre begins, at last, to arrive at its rightful position.

THE APPRENTICE

Adams formed themselves into a species of dramatic censorship, and by turns put down their remarks on the play of the evening, meeting *next* evening" [the italics are unaccountably Dunlap's] "to criticize the critique, and give it passport to the press."

Dunlap sideswipes Mr. Adams as being a member of the group not through his attainments but "only distinguished as being the son and brother of Presidents of the United States" and explains that the young men signed initials to the reviews, the only clue to the authorship being in the last initial, which was usually the initial of the actual author. The youngsters played pretty deadly pranks upon Dunlap, now and then, by using an occasional "D," thereby hinting hilariously that he had written the pieces himself. "The rogues," says Dunlap, "intended to throw some credit on the writer of this work."

Washington Irving, signing himself Jonathan Oldstyle, emerged with the turn of the nineteenth century and began poking salutary fun at the methods of the theatre and the behavior of the audiences. After ridiculing the awkwardness of a group of supers, he suggested that the management try to get them off the stage thereafter by way of a trap door under each man. His description of an audience in 1801 is exuberant, and would be almost unbelievable if his report of coöperative rudeness were not corroborated by many observers.

"I was much amused," he wrote, "by the humor and waggery of the gallery which, by the way, is kept in excellent order by the constables who are stationed there. The noise in this part of the house is somewhat similar to that which prevailed in

Noah's Ark; for we have the imitation of the whistles and yells of every kind of animal. This, in some measure, compensates for the want of music, as the gentlemen of our orchestra are very economic of their favors."

It took pretty forcible acting to subdue such unruly patrons and the actors had to dominate or quit. But, as Mr. Moses remarks in his study of American dramatists, "The palmy days of acting were the trashy days of drama."

The theatre was awake critically before it was creatively.

Dunlap sensed the problem that confronted native dramatists when he pointed out that the contemporary authors had not matured "Their notions of the result of the great political changes which had taken place, to know how far to assert independence in literature or government, or how far to imitate their European ancestors." Dunlap couldn't do it himself, but he understood what ought to be done.

The deficiencies were more thoroughly analyzed and the goal more clearly stated by James K. Paulding in *The American Quarterly Review*. Writing with much prescience in 1827 he said:

"By a national drama we mean not merely a class of dramatic productions written by Americans, but one appealing to the national feeling—founded upon domestic incidents—illustrating or satirizing domestic manners and, above all, displaying a generous chivalry in the maintenance and vindication of those great and illustrious peculiarities of situation and character by which we are distinguished from all other nations."

In a pioneering nation those "illustrious peculiarities" are

34

bound to exhibit themselves first in externals. It takes time for something of a nation's inner truth to emerge; it takes time for it to find its authentic gesture. The gawky actors of Irving's joke, the rude audiences, the sentimentality, the strength, the idealism, vulgarity, and passionate insularity are all a part of it. Here were the ingredients of a great experiment. No dramatist, short of indubitable genius, could have seized on the aspects of a nation in flux, and wrought out of such materials the enduring stuff of dramatic literature. America was not, at that moment, giving birth to dramatic genius. But it was beginning to wonder why.

It is fair, I think, to point out that even in the older societies of Europe dramatic genius was not exactly epidemic at the time. Goethe, it is true, was toiling on the one indisputable masterpiece of the period, and the French theatre was verging into the revolt against classicism with *"Hierro!"* for the password. England, preoccupied with the rising novelist, the Cockney poets, and the burgeoning spirit of Empire, let the theatre dwindle to an arena of acting. In Russia, Gogol with Pushkin's prompting, was cutting the farcical capers of *Revizor* and dislodging the dramatic pebble that was to become a political avalanche. The world was turning a corner it didn't see until it looked back.

America was bringing forth artists but they were not interested in the theatre. New England was, in Van Wyck Brooks's word, flowering, but apart from a few stilted and wholly undramatic pieces by Longfellow, the major literary figures held hands off. Poe, when he touched the theatre at all, did so from a critic's arm's length, instead of giving to it what was undoubtedly and by both heredity and talent a magnificent sense of dramatic narrative. His one play, *Politian* (which he accused Longfellow of borrowing for *The Spanish Student*), proved of no lasting importance.

Unlike other arts the drama is never any greater than the need a people have for it. Other arts may continue competently, if not brilliantly, in the tradition of a period, but in the theatre the lack of creative energy presents immediately an hiatus during which the playhouses may continue to function as places of entertainment, but emptily. Compared, for instance, to the contemporary growth of the Hudson River and White Mountain schools of painting, uninspired, perhaps, but solidly grounded, the drama in the new world was nowhere. Small wonder that it was an actor's theatre. It had to be that or nothing.

Though it must have been difficult for them to admit it the chief actors of the time felt the urgent need for native plays and did what they could to encourage American playwrights. Edwin Forrest, who was as popular then as any movie star or baseball hero is now, and who had, by his affront to Macready in Edinburgh precipitated the fatal riot in Astor Place on May 7, 1849, was one of the first to offer a prize for playwrighting. The usual offer was $500, a good deal in those days of open piracy, and James Wallack topped everyone with the offer of a thousand. The urgency of these actor appeals was as great, almost, as if they were offering a reward for the return of the drama, dead or alive. As things turned out, alas! it was usually dead.

One of Forrest's offers will suggest the extremity. Its historical value, such as it is, lies in the fact that it brought forward one of the most famous native plays of the time. Here is what he wrote to an editor:

"Dear Sir,—Feeling extremely desirous that dramatic letters should be more cultivated in my native country, and believing that the dearth of writers in that department is rather the result of a want of the proper incentive than of any deficiency of requisite talents, I should feel greatly obliged to you if you would communicate to the public, in the next number of the *Critic,* the following offer. To the author of the best tragedy, in five acts, of which the hero or principal character shall be an aboriginal of this country, the sum of five hundred dollars, and half the proceeds of the third representation, with my own gratuitious services on that occasion."

The winning play of two hundred submitted was *Metamora,* or the Last of the Wampanoags, forerunner of a series of American Indian plays that were, all things considered, about as vital as Lo, the poor cigar store effigy.

Probably the one potentially important writing talent devoted to the theatre of the early century was John Howard Payne's who, as a young man, had been an exceedingly popular actor in both New York and London but who, in the vagaries of a tumultuous and suspicious temperament, turned into a hack adapter of foreign plays, chiefly from the French, a job he got originally at Drury Lane through the efforts of Lord Byron's ineffable Hobhouse. Both Washington Irving and Charles Lamb, close friends of Payne's, tried to steady him on a career that was continually upset by a persecution mania, and though he wrote and adapted innumerable plays he is chiefly remembered, if the library shelf can be called memory in the theatre, for *Charles the Second,* in which Irving collaborated, and *Brutus, or the Fall of Tarquin.*

This last is a flamboyant piece, whose published preface frankly acknowledged its obvious derivation from other plays, notably Shakespeare's *Julius Caesar* and *Coriolanus,* but it so aptly fitted the robustious style of acting of the period that Edmund Kean made his great come-back in it in London, and it was for many years a veritable war-horse in the United States for such actors as Forrest and the elder Booth. Payne's immortality is more securely fixed by *Home Sweet Home* which is, in its own way, an adaptation of a Sicilian peasant song.

Payne's playwrighting contemporaries could scarcely be classed above the rank of amateur. Within the best meaning of the term they were lovers of the theatre, or what seems to have passed for the same thing in their estimation, they were lovers of Shakespeare. They were lawyers or doctors, or what not, who took a dilettante interest in writing closet dramas without, for the most part, any immediate intention of performance.

Their subjects were remote in both time and place; none of them was stirred by the events around them, another war with England and the swift expansion of a new Republic. The period is littered with plays of such titles as *The Spanish Exile, Mohammed, De Lara,* or *The Moorish Bride.*

One other of Forrest's prize plays deserves mention because it provided its star with a typical vehicle, Robert T. Conrad's

Jack Cade. Unlike most slavish imitators of Shakespeare Judge Conrad (he was also one-time Mayor of Philadelphia) went to his Elizabethan sources, but by yielding to the Kotzebue democratic influences, he dared to adopt a viewpoint of his own on this figure in the insurrection of 1450 in the second part of *Henry VI.*

No wonder Forrest made the rafters ring with the roaring bombast of Conrad's lines. What actor of the time wouldn't have picked the last shred from such speeches as the big identification scene in the final act, when Jack Cade confronts his lordly enemy:

> Ay, but forgot you not, though years and troubles
> Passed darkly o'er him! But thy victim's widow—
> Ha! doth her name appal thee? Thine the arm—
> Coward! That smote her! Thou it was that gave
> Her wasted form to the fierce flames! thou! thou!
> Thought'est thou not of her boy? The poor Jack Cade
> Is now the avenger! Mortimer no more—
> Behold me, Cade the bondman!

Forrest plainly could give such stuff all that the nineteenth century required. One of his biographers, swept into the usual passion which Forrest's partisans seemed to catch by some spiritual contagion, assures us that "Jack Cade was his incarnate tribuneship of the people, the blazing harangue of a later Rienzi, inflamed by more frightful personal wrongs and inspired with a more desperate love of liberty."

39

George Vanderhoff, in *Leaves From an Actor's Note-Book* gives a further sidelight on Forrest, though in *Metamora:*

"His voice surged and roared like the angry sea, lashed into fury by a storm; till, as it reached its boiling, seething climax, in which the serpent hiss of hate was heard, at intervals, amidst its louder, deeper hoarser tones, it was like the falls of Niagara in its tremendous downsweeping cadence: it was a whirlpool, a tornado, a cataract of illimitable rage."

One gathers that Mr. Forrest was an actor. The enduring evidence of the movie may help the theatre to the extent of rendering such descriptions unnecessary—not to say impossible.

Plainly in such plays the actor had to supply the heat and the steam; plainly without the spectacular proceedings of a performance, without the combined vocal abilities of a wind machine, Niagara in spate, and an articulate bull, the dramatic meaning could not have risen above a whisper.

The formula for writing such plays was simple enough, and couldn't have fooled even the authors. All that was needed was a pretty good knowledge of Shakespeare, a memory shrewd enough to avoid exact duplication of phrasing, which might have aroused suspicion, and an actor capable of rolling off empty sonorities as if they meant something. On the audiences the effect was doubtless close to group hypnotism.

Typical of them all, and the best of the midcentury romantic dramatists was George Henry Boker, head and front of the Philadelphia school. A wealthy and cultivated young man who had gone in for poetry quite heavily at Princeton, he was chief figure in the troup which included Bayard Taylor, and something of his attitude towards his time (and towards the theatre as a living instrument) may be glimpsed in a line from a letter to a friend: "Get out of your age as far as you can." The ivory tower can ask no more.

Boker's first play, *Calaynos,* was well received, even in England; his second, *Anne Boleyn,* was never produced, and his third, *The Betrothal,* was so criticized in its London production that Boker promptly blamed the critical slurs on English jealousy. 'Twas ever thus between the cousinly shores of the Atlantic. Possibly England merely felt she had enough in Bulwer-Lytton.

The avoidance of American themes by the foremost dramatic writers of the time was deliberate, and smacked faintly of the intellectual snobbism that led many of the contemporary literary figures Europe-wards.

"There are," Boker wrote in another letter, "no such subjects for historical tragedy on earth as are to be found in the Spanish history of that period." He was referring to the period of Alfonso XII, and his princeling, Peter the Cruel, not exactly subjects of burning local interest to the American theatre of the nineteenth century.

As a man of social position and wealth, sensitive, cultivated, and of subtle humor, Boker had considerable influence in his time, but his most famous play *Francesca da Rimini* seems even now overrated. In the Civil War period he became active in politics, was one of the founders of the Union League Club, and for his valorous support he was sent by Grant as Minister

to Constantinople. Later he was transferred to Russia, where his social distinction was appreciated so greatly that the Czar asked to have him retained in his diplomatic post when administrative changes at Washington brought his term to an end. The Czar knew nothing about democratic spoils.

In a rather naïve letter for a man of his sophistication Boker explains how he wrote 2800 lines in three weeks, and "found little to change."

"The play," he said of his own work, "is more dramatic than former ones, fiercer in its displays of intense passions, and, so far as mere poetry goes, not inferior, if not superior, to any of them."

In spite of the fact that he thought the whole piece "proved tedious" when it was given at the Broadway Theatre in September, 1855, William Winter urged Lawrence Barrett to revive it, and helped him with a new version. It was in this version that Otis Skinner acted with Barrett in Chicago in 1882, and again, with his own company, in 1901.

Doubtless this *Francesca da Rimini* shone in comparison with other Pennsylvania Elizabethans, and though Professor Quinn calls it the supreme creation of the early drama, it is sadly lacking in style of any sort, to say nothing of the high requirements of poetic tragedy. It moves swiftly enough through soundly constructed situations, but even the lullingly imitative blank verse is jarred, now and then, by phrases that seem appallingly commonplace.

While all this high-flown and self-conscious eloquence was occupying the theatre humbler events were shaping towards a more realistic native drama. Irving's *Rip Van Winkle* emerged as the composite work of many hands, and in the performances of Burke and Jefferson it made an imprint on popular taste which continues to this day in what seems to be a preference for erratic, picturesque, and somewhat raffish old men. Rip's legitimate successors in public favor include Lightnin' Bill Jones, Jeeter Lester in *Tobacco Road,* and the two grandpas in *On Borrowed Time* and *You Can't Take It With You.* For a nation of alleged go-getting business men, our national dream prince seems to be a worthless loafer.

As a turning point towards a different theatre we may take Poe's criticism of Mrs. Mowatt's *Fashion.* Here was the American rustic again with heart of purest gold, contrasted with the foibles and the fops of bogus Europeans and their American imitators. Writing in *The Broadway Journal* in April 1845 he declared that if Mrs. Mowatt's comedy succeeded at all (which it did) it would succeed because of "The very carpets, the very ottomans, the very chandeliers, and the very conservatories which gained so decided a popularity for that most inane and most despicable of all modern comedies—the *London Assurance* of Boucicault."

Two years later Walt Whitman was grumbling in the Brooklyn *Eagle* about the state of the theatre, and predicting great things for the man who could knock some sense into it.

"If some bold man," he wrote, "would take the theatre in hand in this country, and resolutely set his face against the starring system, as a system—some *American* it must be, and not moulded in the long established ways of the English stage—

43

if he should take high ground, revolutionize the drama, and discard much that is not fitted to present tastes and to modern ideas—engage and encourage American talent, (a term made somewhat nauseous by the use it has served for charlatans, but still a good term) look above merely the gratification of the vulgar and of those who love glittering scenery—give us American plays, too, matter fitted to American opinions and institutions—our belief is he would do the Republic a service, and himself, too, in the long round."

Five years later he was to get, at least the subject matter, in *Uncle Tom's Cabin,* George L. Aiken's unauthorized dramatic version of Mrs. Stowe's sensationally successful novel. Mrs. Stowe didn't approve of the theatre, and would have none of it. It is worth nothing, I think, that the unsigned critic in the New York *Herald* for September 3, 1852, denounced the play as in bad taste and urged all concerned to drop it.

"It is calculated, if persisted in," he added prophetically, "to become a firebrand of the most dangerous character to the peace of the whole country."

Compared with such authentic pictures of the negro as *Porgy* and *The Green Pastures* in our own time, the Stowe-Aiken stage negro has obvious deficiencies, but he represents a considerable improvement, even over Zeke, in Mrs. Mowatt's *Fashion* and when he is compared to the earlier negro portraits, as Cesar, for instance, in *Jonathan Postfree* he seems a masterpiece. Cesar, around 1807, was saying with something approaching burlesque Orientalism:

"I don't know what ole missee can see in him to make her likee him so much—but I must holee my tongue."

In historical perspective the defects of an artist may seem minimized somewhat if he has managed, to the limit of his ability, to keep alive an interest in his art. On that basis Dion Boucicault may be exonerated to some extent for his fabulous claptrap. Even contemporary critics condemned his seemingly inexhaustible supply of plays, borrowed from everywhere, but the sheer energy and spirit of this Dubliner of French descent, who dominated the American stage in the middle of the century, did hold a public interest.

With his ascendancy the theatre passed definitely into the realm of sentimental melodrama, patterned largely on French models, and it was to stay there, for all Daly and the others could do about it, until Ibsen and Zola were to rescue it. Professor Quinn still seems to deplore Ibsen's subject matter and Arthur Hopkins has lately doubted whether Ibsen effected a rescue so much as an execution. Possibly the drama moves, as a man does when he walks, by a series of coordinated stumbles. In correcting one tendency it inclines too far in the other direction. Its moments of perfect balance can be only moments of genius—or stagnation. Something is always the matter with it; it is, in fact, always dying. The depth of its meaning to us lies in the fact that it never quite does.

Something of Boucicault's influence in keeping it alive in a stuffy atmosphere may be gauged from a brief tabulation of his most successful plays, and the number of their performances:

London Assurance, 2,900 times; *The Colleen Bawn,* 3,100 times; *The Streets of New York,* 2,800; *The Corsican Brothers,* 2,200; *Arrah-na-Pogue,* 2,400; *The Octoroon,* 1,800 times. They are all figures to make most modern managers weep with envy.

Charles Reade, with whom he collaborated, wrote of Boucicault:

"Like Shakespeare and Molière the beggar steals everything he can lay his hands on; but he does it so deftly, so cleverly that I can't help condoning the theft."

Boucicault knew what he was about, and set out on the well tried theory of pleasing the public. The clamor for his work was so great that a play was in rehearsal before the ink was dry. How could a man in such haste take time to put the blotter to some of his soupier sentimentalities? Boucicault was a true workman of the theatre, and cared for no aspects of it which carried him away from the stage itself. He contended that acting could be taught only on the platform, as swimming is taught in water. He boldly proclaimed that he was interested in the fifty-cent audience and tried to give it its money's worth. He was ahead of his time. He would have been the super-giant-colossus of an undreamed-of medium, the absolute czar of Hollywood. He was a movie genius without a roll of film to his name. To him the story and the effects were everything, and he went straight to his business, with no bother about subtleties, inner meanings, or complexities of character.

For forty-nine of the sixty-eight years of his lifetime he was active in the theatre not only as author, but as manager, lecturer and teacher. When he was attacked for his methods of playwrighting and accused of ignorance he either shrugged off the attack, or confounded his critics with sweeping assertions of his own theory.

"The essence of a rule," he wrote, "is its necessity. It must be reasonable and always in the right. The unities of time and place do not seem to be reasonable, and have been violated with impunity, therefore are not always in the right. The liberty of imagination should not be sacrificed to arbitrary restrictions and traditions that lead to dullness and formality. Art is not a church; it is the philosophy of pleasure."

Besides his impulsiveness, his frankly commercial outlook, and his disregard for dramatic literature Boucicault had one other compelling reason for his extravagant output. He was an early champion of copyright reform, and insisted on a royalty basis of payment. When he was unable to persuade managers in England and the United States to this course he organized companies of his own and took a percentage of the receipts for his commission. This practice seriously affected the prevailing stock system but it should certainly be given part of the credit for the later legal protection of author's rights.

Coming on the heels of the closet dramatists Boucicault brought back to the theatre something of its essential spirit. It is too bad that his pen was dipped in grease paint more often than in ink, and worse still that a corrective occasionally dims the value of its own work. His effect on the theatre was out of all proportion to the value of his plays—if they can even be considered his plays. He borrowed from many sources, but his energy was his own, and he put it into the American theatre when that quality, among many others, was sorely needed.

Boucicault lived until 1890 and was active (even matrimonially) almost to the end of his life. At the moment of his death he was collaborating on a play with Bret Harte, and he had laid the basis for a proxy influence on the theatre by aiding the career of David Belasco, who was, for a time, Boucicault's secretary. When there is no dramatist around it is just as well for the theatre to have a good showman.

The modern American drama begins, according to Professor Quinn, with Augustin Daly. Immediately after the Civil War there had been the usual attempt to capitalize recent history, and there were numerous pieces using the war for background.

Mr. Moses's picture of the theatre-going taste of the eighteen-seventies, in *The American Dramatist* is sound, and not very flattering:

"It fed itself," he wrote, "on romantic dreams, on love of class distinction in a country where no class was supposed to exist. It dared nothing for the craft of the theatre. The playhouse was a stunt, not an organism; the emotional quality of the actor was what counted. The relish was for just the kind of melodrama the French dramatists were turning out. The heightened emotion of Dumas *fils,* the sentimentality of Robertson, the scenic efforts of Daly's *The Streets of New York,* or of *The Two Orphans*—lords and ladies, bandits, wronged innocence—this was the food (of the seventies). To it was brought the most superlative acting of a certain type; the acting

48

that threw emotion in the face to blind one to the crudities of expression, of motive, of story."

It was this public that was daydreaming while the foundations of industrial feudalism was being laid under its nose; this public, that within a hundred years of its political independence had gone through three wars, and explored and exploited a continent. It probably felt like sitting back in the sultry comforts of hothouse Victorianism, and taking its ease; but it is an everlasting pity it did. That moment of relaxation set us back. Like the newly rich we were, we took our ease too soon—and for granted. The theatre was just another toy among the pretty trinkets of a bright new world which had its work to do.

The statement that the modern American drama begins with Daly demands some explanation when it is considered that during his long career as a very able manager, he produced chiefly adaptations of German and French plays. But he was driven to these, in some measure, when his repeated efforts to encourage native playwrights met with repeated failure. He continually urged Bret Harte, William Dean Howells, Mark Twain and Henry James to write for the theatre, and accurately gauged the taste of the times for domestic characters.

"It was indispensable," he wrote about the German plays he had adapted for American audiences, "when preparing them for the stage with any hope of pleasing my patrons, to do away entirely with one or more German characters and fill the place with an American type which my audience would all know and would applaud."

Until Daly's time men of literary eminence could not be

persuaded to take an interest in playwrighting because of the standards of production, because their work was unprotected by copyright and because the theatre had no interest in any quality beyond the effectiveness of a work on the platform.

Daly, as a man of cultivated tastes, much above the run-of-the-mill manager, created confidence in his theatre by organizing an able company of actors and setting a high standard of production. Through his enterprise and sound practice he succeeded in establishing his own theatre in London, and even invaded the Continental theatre with an English-speaking company.

Here was a man who set some store by the theatre as an art, who knew that American drama need not be a matter of American subjects and American history, and yet found himself baffled by the reluctance of literary artists to subject themselves to the rigorous demands of stage writing. Of the group Howells made what may be considered the only permanent contributions, and indeed, Professor Quinn goes so far as to hold that he is "surpassed by no one who has written in English in the creation of the farce comedy which depends for its effect upon the delicate contrast of domestic and social values."

There is an undeniable humorous charm to much of his dialogue and a sense of mischief that seems derived from Gilbert. Perhaps his position as a creative dramatist may be established in the future, but at the moment his chief effect on the theatre would seem to have been through his critical writings, in his recognition of Edward Harrigan as authentic native talent, for his encouragement of Herne and Fitch, and for his championship of the cause of realism.

He hailed Harrigan's art as "the art of Goldoni" and he saw in its picture of low life (though whether it is essentially lower than fashionable life is another question) the promise of important work, "the spring of true American comedy."

Daly and Boucicault had both taken notice of the rise of city types, but Harrigan was to stamp them with the imprint of his own talent. Where Boucicault had exalted the native Irishman, and laid claim, in fact, to creating the Irish drama (to what must have been the later horror of Yeats and Lady Gregory) Harrigan depicted the immigrant, and by way of contrast added the character of Gustave Luchmuller the German butcher, for all the hilarious brawling that is perpetuated in such racial quarrels as *Potash and Perlmutter* and *Abie's Irish Rose*. He added also a negro type, but even Howells took exception to this as being one-sided since, he said, "they are of the gloomy, razor-bearing variety, full of short-sighted lies and prompt dishonesties, amusing always, but truculent and tricky; and the sunny sweetness which we all know in negro character is not there."

Bridging the latter half of the nineteenth century were three men, any one of whom might have become the dominant figure in American drama. They were, in the order of their appearance on the birth records, James A. Herne, Bronson Howard, and Steel Mackaye. Mackaye was the shortest-lived, and though he had, in many ways, as much, if not more promise than either of the others, time was against him.

Time was, in fact, against all three. Born within four years of one another, Herne in 1839, Howard in '42, and Mackaye in '44, they labored under the same handicap. Through their maturing years they felt the impulses against romanticism which set in after the Civil War, and while Herne and Howard lived to see the realistic theatre, neither was quite able to shake off the deadening weight of their earlier period.

Mackaye seems to have deserved more of the historians than they have given him. He was a serious theatre workman, a man who took on his job as a professional, and who revealed not only an imaginative insight into his own time, but coupled this with considerable daring. He was an innovator at a moment when it was a good deal easier to let the drama take its stilted course. He championed the Delsarte methods of naturalism in acting, boldly experimented in staging technique even with duplex stages, and more than any other playwright of the period realized the sociological influence of the drama. At a moment when the drama took on any complexion profitable at the box office he saw its political weight, and recognized its value as an instrument for liberalism.

Unhappily his play of the French Revolution *Paul Kauvar* reveals the deadening effect of the romantic drama, though there are stretches in its dialogue, as in the earlier *Hazel Kirke* that plainly reveal its author's inclination towards realistic treatment.

It is in his own comment on the play, however, that he reveals what potentialities were lost in his untimely death.

"I became conscious," he told an interviewer, "that certain

foreign ideas—the natural outgrowth of excessive poverty and despotism in the Old World—were insinuating themselves into the hearts and minds of American laborers to an extent perilous to their own prosperity and to the very life of the Republic.

"In this country political corruption and the grasping spirit of corporations are constantly affording the demagogue or the dreamer opportunity to preach the destruction of civil order with great plausibility, giving scope to reckless theorists who have so often, in the world's history, baffled the endeavors of the rational and patient liberalists of their day."

His personal courage in backing up this attitude is shown by his championship of some Chicago anarchists who had been condemned to death. He was totally out of sympathy with the men, but felt that the preservation of the legal system was more important than any issue of immediate wrongdoing.

More by his personal record, I admit, than in the value of his dramatic work Steele Mackaye gives the impression of being the first American dramatist to have his eyes open, to see the world he lived in with vivid insight and a valiant spirit. If he had lived we could use such a man.

Though he lacked Mackaye's serious outlook Bronson Howard doubtless understood his time better than his plays indicate. His intentions were lighter, and in his early work he readily borrowed the foreign models so liberally sprinkled on the American boards. Mr. Moses says that he once confessed "how one of his earliest manuscripts contained speeches in which Newport people went about exclaiming 'Egad.'"

Even in his most popular period his American characters

53

were frequently disclosed in European atmosphere, and though there is no denying the fact that he was a pioneer in many respects, he suffers the retrospective fate of many pioneers in the wonder why he didn't go further. His *Shenandoah* on a Civil War theme, while immensely popular, is interesting now chiefly as a forerunner of Gillette's *Secret Service. Baron Rudolph* revealed his knowledge (in 1881) of the elements of struggle between capital and labor, and *The Henrietta* sounded the overture for the American business man play.

Thus it is obvious that his subjects were timely, and he deserves all credit for handling them. It must be remembered, too, that he began his work when the managers were skeptical about American playwrights, and in adhering to the French models he was, as he thought, cutting his cloth in the most acceptable fashion. It is a pity, part, in fact, of the triple pity which Brander Matthews expressed when he said that the riper development of the American drama of Howard's period was retarded by three untoward events—"the premature deaths of Clyde Fitch and William Vaughn Moody, and the premature birth of Bronson Howard."

From the unlikeliest beginnings Herne wrought a career that was astounding in its effects. With only the scantiest formalities of education he went on the stage in San Francisco, where he was associated with young Belasco, had the actor's usual fling at Boucicault (as who could avoid him) and made his own version of *Rip Van Winkle* in which he played.

After acting for many years in the usual heroic parts he found himself, at the age of thirty-nine, under three influences which propelled him towards a unique position in American play-wrighting. His second wife, Miss Katherine Corcoran, seems to have inspired him to constructive rebellion against the play-wrighting he despised; David Belasco persuaded him that he had high talents as a dramatist, and finally, and most power-fully, Mr. Howells, then championing realism with all his might as editor of *The Atlantic Monthly* and in his own work, gave Herne the final impetus.

It was Howells who was bewailing the imitative instinct of the average American writer, and declaring that "he is in-structed to idealize his personages, that is, to take the lifelike-ness out of them and put the booklikeness into them."

"Now," he added, speaking of Herne, "we are beginning to see and to say that no author is an authority, except in those moments when he held his ear close to Nature's lips and caught her very accents."

Beyond these influences were two others, possibly of equal weight, though there is no way of estimating their effect. Herne was closely familiar with Ibsen's plays (though I believe only the happy ending version of *A Doll's House* had been played in America at that time) and he was a friend of Henry George, author of that earth-shaking *Progress and Poverty* and the man who made such a deep impression on another rising dramatic figure of the time, the red-bearded George Bernard Shaw.

Three contemporary opinions are, perhaps, most significant in estimating Herne's achievement.

Of *Margaret Fleming* Mr. Howells wrote:

"The power of this story, as presented in Mr. Herne's everyday phrase . . . was terrific. It clutched the heart. It was common; it was pitilessly plain; it was ugly, but it was true, and it was irresistible."

Of *Griffith Davenport,* when it was acted in London by Mr. and Mrs. Herne, William Archer wrote:

"I felt throughout that here I was in the presence of what I had come to seek, and had not found elsewhere—original American art. And America, to its indelible discredit, failed to recognize it."

The third is inevitable. William Winter denounced Herne's plays for their "prosy literalism" and refused to admit him to a higher category than "respectable mediocrity."

Archer was Ibsen's translator and champion; Winter his most vehement critical antagonist, always excepting Clement Scott. Just as Ibsen followed the scribe pattern up to a point, and then twisted it to his own purpose, so Herne did with the formula plays to which he had given his younger days on the American stage. Here was the issue and here the battle. The American theatre was at last taking from Europe something besides a manner and a prattle. Here was an idea, and it takes an idea to make the theatre live. America was beginning to feel its way towards a drama of its own.

MATURITY

CHAPTER III

MATURITY

Bᴜᴛ ɪʙsᴇɴ ᴡᴀs ɴᴏᴛ ᴛʜᴇ ᴏɴʟʏ ɪɴғʟᴜᴇɴᴄᴇ which was slowly but powerfully bearing down upon the American stage. Other forces were moving throughout Europe to reshape the theatre, and to bring about a renaissance. A new idea was moving not only in the playwright but in the medium of his work to evolve the "new stagecraft." Simultaneously, as if by a prearranged signal, the theatre all over Europe was in revolt.

A few French critics had struggled upstairs to a dingy theatre

59

run by a clerk in the gas company, and had had their eyes opened, by Antoine, to the *Theatre Libre*. Appia had announced his theories of stage production, and these had been taken up and expanded and ballyhooed by Gordon Craig. Reinhardt had emerged in Germany, Shaw, Pinero, and Jones in England, and, under the stimulus of Lady Gregory and Yeats, the Irish theatre was burgeoning with new life. In Russia Stanislavsky and Nemirovitch-Dantchenko, influenced strongly by the work of the Duke of Saxe-Meinigen, were founding, in the Moscow Art Theatre, the greatest acting instrument of the time, and discovering in an obscure doctor named Chekhov a man who was to put an indelible mark upon the world theatre. The giant from the north had brought in his train such dramatists as Hauptmann, Strindberg, Schnitzler, Gorki, Tolstoi and Sudermann.

No one who has ever pieced together the history of the theatre has failed to note the danger of generalizations. It is difficult to assign a reason for this sudden outbreak of the theatre in so many places, this widespread recrudescence in a neglected art. Hugo and the romanticists had carried the day against the classic rigidities but their reign was scarcely more than a stopgap before the onrush of dramatic realism.

Larger forces than merely a revolution in art were doubtless at the bottom of the overturn. Science was slowly but inexorably cutting under the structure of faith; mechanical invention, industrial expansion and economic dependence were reducing the importance of the individual to a standardized unit in the impersonal level of a civilization whose knowledge had swiftly passed beyond its powers of organization.

Against this suppression of the individual the revolt was aimed, and it carried with it all the cults of self-expression. In the scale of things every man was as important as any other, and he had the right to his own life. The doctors, the philosophers, and the poets all said so. Life was no longer a matter of romantic daydreams gratified in the misty reflection of heroic grandeur. It had been scaled down to make every man a hero. The details of his existence became impressive for no other reason than that they were average. The truth of these details became an aim that elbowed all other aims out of the way. Truth excused anything, even, finally, its own irrelevance; because one detail was as meaningful as another, and in the cult of accuracy, the photographic became the ideal, selectivity was gone, and realism reduced to the stupid literalism of mere copying. Before reaction set in it was to go as far in its physical aspects as Belasco's putting $30,000 worth of real antique furniture on the stage, and another producer's fumigating his audience with the smell of frying onion merely because the scene of his play was a lunch wagon. At the opposite extreme Pirandello was to make the idea of realism the basis for a new challenge on the nature of reality itself, raising thereby the whole issue of the theatre's intent in the realm of illusion.

The new stagecraft had already gone into the matter by its refusal to submit to the convention of the fourth wall, and the picture frame stage. Through a maze of theories of constructivism, expressionism, and impressionism, through an increasingly dramatic use of light, through its insistence that the actor appear "in the round" naturally, without the trickery of false perspectives, the new school carried the theatre away from the old formulas, and freed it to move in any direction it pleased with its problem determined only by the nature of the play itself.

But the effects of this European revolution were not immediately felt in America, chiefly because the managerial system then in power was conservative and entrenched. The theatrical producers were simply interested in marketing a commodity, and were not particularly interested, beyond certain improving standards of quality, in its nature.

The Frohmans, as the dominant producing firm in New York, frankly admitted as much. "I do believe," said Charles Frohman, "that throughout the United States a play really requires a star artist, man or woman,—woman for choice."

An astute showman, intelligent and of high integrity, Frohman did much to raise the producing standards in America, but within the commercial limitations of giving the public what it wanted. Or what he thought it wanted. The public takes time, sometimes, to make up its mind.

Unhappily this tardy acceptance of "the new theatre" had a crippling influence on two of the most promising talents of Frohman's day—Augustus Thomas and Clyde Fitch.

Both had admirable abilities, and in differing directions, both were capable of shrewd observation. They revealed a common interest in American locales, but Thomas had a much stronger sense of it than Fitch, whose characters and point of view, regardless of the scene of his drama, remained definitely of New York.

Neither was able to avoid altogether the lingering influences of the old melodramas, though both of them were sufficiently caught up in the movement towards realism to free their dialogue, for the most part, from the rigidities of the past. Their dialogue is less strained than any American dialogue before it, less awkward, and more to the point.

Their trouble, as both of them realized, was the star system, and its demand for the tailor-made play. With a good deal of amused urbanity, in fact, Mr. Thomas described how he cut the pattern and fitted the cloth of one of his plays to the personality of Nat Goodwin, and explained why, given such a star, the play had to take on a certain tone, and followed a certain routine.

As for Fitch he was acutely aware of the burden:

"O! M.M." he wrote to Margaret Merington (author of *Captain Letterblair* a vehicle for E. H. Sothern). "What a state it is when there is only *one man* to whom one can offer a play and expect to have it in any ½ adequate way presented—I mean of course a play and not a star's piece. I tell you there will never be good American dramatists until there are good American producers. And without these last mentioned gentlemen, the good American dramatists that there are—you and me, *par example,* can never do ourselves justice."

Fitch's position in American dramatic literature has never been fairly settled. Among critics old enough to have seen his plays in their original production, and what is more important, with the surrounding atmosphere of American society of that day, they hold, undoubtedly, a higher value than they deserve. But there is a strong tendency—especially at the moment, when there is a faint suspicion in some quarters that any character on the stage who wears a collar button is a dirty capitalist and therefore useless—there is a tendency, I say, to minimize his achievements.

Yet it seems that, accepting his plays on their own terms, as society drama, they fall considerably short of their obligations. They reveal, it is true, a fidelity to detail, and an occasional sharp commentary on social manners and customs, but it is obvious that they are more concerned with personality than with character and that the comment goes no deeper than a smartly superficial humor.

The current scorn for comedies of manners is, of course, indefensible since any given state of society as a whole can be illuminated from any level, and given value, provided the terms are clear. As a modern dramatist Fitch had the first, and perhaps the last opportunity to create a real social comedy because he had the unique opportunity to observe society when it was in the state that is indispensable for highest comedy development. I mean that he lived at a time when the apparent stability of the world freed the comedy of manners from any other consideration, whereas in the present more complex, more heterogeneous and altogether miscellaneous state of that society, there is no basis, or very little basis, for such comedy. That, at the moment, is the chief difficulty of such an admirable comic dramatist as S. N. Behrman, whose observation is stricter than

Fitch's, whose spirit is more compassionate, but whose material is sadly disarranged by the general plight. It is difficult to write a comedy of manners about a state of chaos.

It appears, in library retrospection, that Langdon Mitchell far exceeded his contemporaries in his contribution to the drama by writing what seems to me to be the first authentically American comedy of manners and giving it the necessary preservative of style. Though it labors under the handicap of one of the worst titles ever recorded in the Copyright Bureau *The New York Idea* is an altogether amusing play, written with a fine sense of discrimination and an unfaltering sense of humor. Unlike most of its coetaneans in the drama it avoided, with great prescience, the use of slang (excepting only one word) so that it has none of the verbal jolts, and antimacassar witticisms that mar others of the period, since nothing seems more faded than slang that has just gone out of fashion and is not yet old enough to be quaintly antique.

Though it was tailored for Mrs. Fiske, and apparently fitted her bright, darting comedy sense to perfection, it is no slavish star vehicle in the ordinary sense. The characters are all deftly and gaily drawn, and they move flawlessly through situations which are forever on the giddiest verge of farce, and yet somehow never slip over the line.

It had by no means the success of Mitchell's *Becky Sharp*, which he did earlier for Mrs. Fiske, or *Pendennis* which he did later for John Drew. His only other play, *The New Marriage*, met with failure in 1911, and Mr. Mitchell during a long lifetime made no further original contributions to the drama. In fact, from his public utterance, seemed to despair of any cultivated public for art in America. It was a flash in the pan; but a flash.

The decade between 1905 and 1915 brought a decided shift among commercial managers to the American play. With the advent of the Shuberts and the warfare with the Syndicate, the theatre began a forced expansion, dictated largely by its financial interests, and we have the period of the "well-made play," most of them mediocre, but native—if that was any consolation. High hopes of all sorts were raised and dashed.

William Vaughn Moody began with celestial visions of poetic drama (which were never produced) and the popular achievements of *The Great Divide* and *The Faith Healer*. Percy Mackaye, with much of his father's insurgence about him, and an equal inheritance of visionary daring, attempted the establishment of spectacles and pageantry with a certain attempt to link such an idea of the theatre with civic and sociological purposes. Very little came of that.

For at this point the theatre was feeling pressure from many quarters, both artistic and commercial. Within the decade the number of playhouses in New York was doubled, and ten years later doubled again. Meanwhile "the road" was steadily shrinking. According to figures compiled by *The Dramatic Mirror* the number of plays on tour declined from an average of 308 between the years 1900 and 1904 to 68 between the years 1925 and 1927. This was due, as I have already pointed out, partly to the mismanagement of the producers, and their mistreatment of both actors and public, and partly to the increase in

66

railroad rates, but most of all because of the cheaper and more popular competition of the movies.

The effect on the theatre, however, was to drive it back on New York, and New York was becoming more and more European. It looked eastward across the Atlantic, instead of backwards on the country from which it is nominally separated only by water. Reinhardt's *Sumurun* was a landmark, as definite in its influence as the Armory Show was in painting, and presently came the Diaglieff Ballet Russe. In a wave of aesthetic jitters the Little Theatre movement was started and astute professionals actually quivered at the thought of a country bursting open with art at every seam. Their fears were not very well grounded, and I shall presently revert to them.

For a date intervenes, and though I daresay none of the Broadway gentlemen spent a sleepless night worrying about a small production of what they took for a group of amateurs on East Fifty-Seventh Street, that out-of-the-way event shook a good many pedestals before its earthquake quieted down. That was the Bandbox Theatre, where a movie house now stands, and it housed a group calling itself the Washington Square Players. Among them were Robert Edmond Jones, Philip Moeller, Edward Goodman, and Helen Westley, and they had scarcely got their curtain up when the War made them put it down again. When their theatre came back, neatly reorganized, it was the Theatre Guild.

More remote, and less direct in its influence, but more profound in its ultimate effect, was an even smaller event that year of 1915 on a porch in Provincetown, when a group of summer colony artists, mostly from Greenwich Village, produced a play by Susan Glaspell, with scene designs by Jones. The next year they had a little better shelter, and a little better playwright, since on the bill of one-actors was a piece called *Bound East For Cardiff* and another called *Thirst* both by Eugene Gladstone O'Neill. The author played the part of the negro in the latter play, and presently when the group got hold of an old stable in Macdougal street, in New York, he came along with them. He came along, and later on moved uptown and across the world.

Almost at the outset O'Neill revealed himself to be a dramatist of larger calibre than any of his native predecessors, a man of deep emotional feeling, observing life not at second hand, as so many others have done, both before and since he set to work, and with the true dramatist's courage in experiment. He has refused to yield to the conventional restrictions of the theatre; has, indeed, been impatient of them. He has boldly declared that he doesn't care if the theatre fails to solve the physical difficulties his plays frequently present, and in one of them at least, *Lazarus Laughed,* he had imposed such a burden on the chief actor that it has never had a professional production.

He has stretched the playing time from the usual two hours and a half to twice, and nearly three times that length. He has put his characters in masks, frankly borrowed the old-fashioned aside as an almost novelistic convention to reveal the psychological state of his characters, and in an experiment with musical rhythms he has taken the Greek drama and given it the modern overtones of psychoanalysis by using the conventionalized portico setting, and then, for his sharpest motives, pryed behind it, physically as well as spiritually, to get at the personal impulses that move his characters.

His beginning with the one-act form gave him a sound basis for theatrical impact, and when he utilized the medium successfully, especially in *The Long Voyage Home* of the Glencairn Cycle, the result was a dramatic flash of tremendous intensity. The one-act play demands precision, speed, a certain degree of style, and in its most powerful phases, the unerring punch of a vaudeville turn. It was an instrument perfectly suited to the quick brutalities of his sardonic dramas, and he used it brilliantly for the remorseless sea stuff he wrought into his early days.

At first glance these shorter pieces seemed to be the work of a vivid reporter, photographic and direct. This was realism —and no doubt—and immensely effective, but O'Neill's growth pushed him further. The surface truth was not enough; he was in quest of a deeper meaning; he would probe the mystery behind external reality.

Of one of his less successful experiments, *The Great God Brown,* he said in a letter of my own prompting:

"It is mystery—the mystery that any man or woman can feel but not understand as the meaning of any event—or accident —in any life on earth. And it is this mystery I want to realize in the theatre. The solution, if there is any, will probably have to be reduced to a test tube, and turn out to be discouragingly undramatic."

As far as it is related to life O'Neill realizes that this mystery is essentially tragical. Like Moody (in his two unproduced poetic dramas) he continually explores man against his fate, but he has steadily expanded the scope of his inquiry, without varying (except in the genial reminiscence of *Ah, Wilderness!*) from the theme of frustration. He uses the same pattern over and over again, the pattern that he used first in *The Long Voyage Home,* and his stage is littered with beaten humanity.

"I'll write about happiness" he once wrote Barrett H. Clark, "if I can happen to meet up with that luxury, and find it sufficiently dramatic and in harmony with any deep rhythm of life. I know that there is more of it in one real tragedy than in all the happy-ending plays ever written. It's mere present day judgment to think of tragedy as unhappy...I don't love life because it's pretty. I am a truer lover than that. I love it naked. There is beauty to me even in its ugliness."

O'Neill's pattern for this is, as I said, *The Long Voyage Home* which concerns a Swedish seaman who is quitting the sea and taking a drink in a waterfront bar, before setting out for his dream—a farm in Sweden. He is drugged and shanghaied back to his ship.

These knock-out drops in one form or another are repeatedly administered to O'Neill characters up and down the list of his plays; proving that the author, with the occasional help of Fate, is pretty inexorable if not, now and then, melodramatic. That is the pattern of *Beyond the Horizon, The Fountain, Desire Under the Elms* and *The Great God Brown,* though it is greatly to O'Neill's credit that he presses closer and closer to the inner meaning of it, and moves away from the more obvious externals. *Strange Interlude* is the beginning of his maturer manner, "a milestone," as Gilbert Gabriel had the sagacity to call it, "to cleave the skyline of the future," and though O'Neill lapsed into the period of *Dynamo* (which was to be the first of a trilogy) and *Days Without End* he came through the authentic masterpiece of *Mourning Becomes Electra*.

For purposes of distinction in rather loose terminology O'Neill's preoccupation is not with the drama of revolt so much as with the drama of acceptance. His conflict goes through various phases—man against a blind fate (*The Long Voyage Home*) man against nature, (*The Fountain* and *Dynamo*) and finally man against himself, which is simply another way of narrowing the mystery down to its sharpest focus and setting a capstone on all the realistic drama's passionate concern for the individual.

In mood, which is invariably the key to O'Neill's writing, he carries this exploration from the tone of violent, but futile resentment through one of mystical paganism, to, finally, a basis of faith in intellectual understanding. The business, as the naturalist Burroughs put it, of "accepting the universe." The progress of this development need not be concerned with his two disastrous examinations of the theme *Dynamo* and the sawdust trail aspects of *Days Without End*.

At whatever point his work is examined, however, it reveals a powerful sense of mysticism, the convenient acceptance, for instance, of Ponce de Leon, tricked to death on the edge of his fabled Fountain of Youth, who cries "I begin to know eternal youth. I have found my fountain. Oh, Fountain of Eternity, take back this drop, my soul."

Or the chant of Cybel, the Earth Mother, in *The Great God Brown:*

"Always Spring comes again, bearing life! Always again! Always, always, forever again!—Spring again—life again—summer and fall and death and peace again! but always, always, love and conception and birth and pain again—Spring bearing the intolerable chalice of life again!—bearing the glorious, blazing crown of life again!"

For two other contrasting examples, take Old Cabot's grim threnody in *Desire Under the Elms:*

"It's a-goin' t'be lonesomer now than ever it war afore—an' I'm gittin' old, Lord,—ripe on the bough. Waal—what d'ye want? God's lonesome, hain't He? God's hard and lonesome."

And from *Marco Millions:*

"Be immortal," says the Great Kahn, taking the words out of O'Neill's mouth. "Be immortal because life is immortal. Contain the harmony of womb and grave within you. Possess life as a lover, then sleep requited in the arms of death. If you awake, love again! If you sleep on, rest in peace. Who knows which? What does it matter? It is nobler not to know."

O'Neill's greatest power lies in this mystical expression. In thought content his plays are not always secure, and their conscious poetry frequently reveals the author at his literary worst. In his religious plays, especially in *Days Without End,* he made the dramatic mistake of reducing such a mystical matter as faith to the realm of intellectual conviction, without pausing to consider that, by its very nature, faith is not a logical conception, capable of demonstration, but a spiritual intuition which needs and can have, no support outside itself.

As an experimenter in dramatic forms O'Neill is tireless. His vivid expansion of the one-act form into a large number of scenes connected with the insistent drum beat of *The Emperor Jones* added immeasurably to the stage effect. His first use of masks in his dramatic version of Coleridge's *The Ancient Mariner* led him into the unexpected incongruity of modern tonsures when his characters' backs were turned. The confusion of identity which occurred in *The Great God Brown* when the personal masks were swapped about among the characters left him undaunted. His trick of the psychological aside in *Strange Interlude* frankly deviated from its original use (where it was legitimate) and deteriorated, in several places, into a vehicle of description which it was his business as a dramatist to put into the action.

O'Neill set up no school and fortunately has no imitators. Yet his is the permeating influence on the American drama, the magnetic pole of the American theatre. For the theatre cannot touch its living functions, as against the revival of its past, without the mouthpiece of a dramatist. O'Neill came along at the urgent moment to use the theatre's newly found freedom in the idiom of his own country, and fortunately, in his own time.

His early use of the one-act medium gave enormous impetus to the Little Theatre movement, that abortive and to my way of thinking, rather silly national excursion into the drama

73

which George Kelly satirized very shrewdly in *The Torch-bearers.*

In the movement's rosy promises, which sound now as if they must have been made under powerful narcotics, we were assured that the little theatres would relieve the country of the commercial incubus of the Broadway managers. In an epidemic of cultural effort community drama clubs, we were told, would cherish the art of the theatre, wrest its leadership from its money-mad jailers, and bring about such a flowering of theatre art that the whole countryside would be dotted with one joyous stage after another. Thereafter, it appeared, Broadway would take its drama from the Little Theatres.

As lately as 1929, when everyone doubted that the Little Theatre would do anything except present free exercise for its assembled egoes, one of its staunchest defenders was cooing, in total defiance of all the facts, that it was, even then, redeeming the drama.

When the Little Theatre movement began to spread, *Variety,* which is the hard-headed business paper of professional amusements, fell into what seems to have been a trance and predicted that "within ten years from now the Little Theatres will have 'the legit' by the throat."

It is apparent now, and has been for a long time, that the Little Theatre never came within throat-grasping distance of anything.

Instead of becoming a pioneer in production, instead of devoting its attention to the possible local development of playwrights, instead, in fact, of doing anything at all constructive, it became a frank imitator of the Broadway theatre, following it slavishly and waiting for its cue.

I would not contend for a moment that any effort to stimulate interest in the theatre in or outside New York is without its merits. It is also true that many of the Little Theatres put on good productions in a manner that compared favorably with the professional stage. It is no affront to call them amateur; this is merely to contend that their amateurishness was not in any creative direction. At a moment when there were between two and three thousand Little Theatres in the country, not one of them, to my knowledge, brought forward in its own production an original play worth noticing.

This would be no reproach if the larger theatre had not, during those years of Little Theatre smugness, done very nicely by regional plays which the Little Theatres should have originated. *Porgy* came out of the South and found production with the Theatre Guild. Mackaye's *This Fine Pretty World*, a drama about the Kentucky mountaineers, whose complicated dialect left a good part of it unintelligible, was done at the world's farthest remove from Kentucky, to wit, the Neighborhood Playhouse in Grand Street. Lulu Vollmer's *Sun-Up, The Shame Woman,* and *The Dunce Boy* had similar metropolitan outlet, as did Virgil Geddes's *The Earth Between,* Lynn Riggs's regional dramas, and Paul Green's *In Abraham's Bosom.*

It was this last named, indeed, which brought about what seems to me final proof of the Little Theatre's timidity in its great challenge to Broadway. It was offered in manuscript before New York production to thirteen Little Theatres, all of

75

which turned it down, but when it won the Pulitzer Prize, after its New York production, the demand for its little theatre production rights almost swamped the publishers.

"If I had a really good experimental play," said the aforementioned Mr. Clark, one of the indefatigable encouragers of native playwrights—speaking, I should judge, more in sorrow than in anger—"if I had a really good experimental play I would try to sell it everywhere on Broadway before I sent it out to the Little Theatres."

Naturally this does not include the college theatres which have developed admirably, and in recent years have done a good deal of constructive work, not only in fostering playwrights but in providing useful channels for beginners to learn their jobs. There are even some honorable, though later-day exceptions among the little theatres themselves, notably the Cleveland and Pasadena playhouses. Nor is the general indictment true of the recent evolution of the summer theatres which have a more professional aspect, which do try to maintain Broadway standards, frequently with Broadway casts; and although their chief value at the moment seems to be in giving a hearing to young actors, they occasionally produce original plays, largely on the basis of a try-out for metropolitan showing, sponsored by the Broadway producer.

Possibly the significant point about all such activity in the American theatre is that it invariably relies on subscriptions. It has done so from earliest times, in the precarious colonial theatres, through the period of Military Thespians, down to the Theatre Guild and the Mercury.

There is an early notice concerning Williamsburg, printed in the Virginia *Gazette* for August 29, 1751:

"Whereas the Company of Comedians that are in New York intend performing in this City, but there being no Room suitable for a Play-House, tis propos'd that a Theatre shall be built by way of Subscription, each Subscriber advancing a Pistole ($3.80) to be entitled to a Box Ticket for the First Night's Diversion."

In theory the subscription theatre is a solution of all the theatre's troubles, but in practice it has obvious, if latent, flaws. It guarantees, of course, an immediate audience of enthusiastic supporters which assists a production over its initial weeks of uncertainty. It is all very well when the subscribers look upon themselves as patrons of an art, but it has been demonstrated that they shift very quickly to patrons of the box office. They want successes. They want, in fact, their money's worth.

By an astute compromise the Theatre Guild has been the single subscription theatre to survive over any appreciable length of time. Once it had weathered its early tribulations and got itself on a firm financial footing it managed, in its best years, to appeal to both the intellectual and pocketbook interests of its customers. For a number of seasons it was unquestionably the most vitalizing influence in the theatre, shrewd enough in its business and in its art to make itself a very profitable pioneer.

But it was by no means, as it is so often assumed, the only enlightened agency at work on Broadway. Such men as Winthrop Ames and Arthur Hopkins and later Brock Pemberton had challenged the leadership of the old school, especially as it was embodied by Belasco. There is not much doubt that Belasco's most imaginative production was himself and I would not for a moment minimize Belasco's genius as a showman. In a subtler fashion, keyed to the special need of his time, he was as great as Barnum and for the same reason. He never lost the Boucicault influence and though a doting and solvent public accepted him for years as a pious esthete, the notion must have made him smile.

Against such self-winding artiness the new groups aimed their attack quite often with no relevant substitute. The Neighborhood Playhouse set up its esthetic output in the unlikely vicinity of Grand Street under the benevolent auspices of the Misses Lewishon. Grand Street seemed more surprised than anyone and, perhaps, showed its deepest interest one night when an expectant mother, mistaking its Settlement mission, was sidetracked from the box office to a maternity ward in what turned out to be the nick of time. When the movement was disbanded it seemed that the Neighborhood Playhouse was remembered chiefly for its production of *The Dybbuk* and its inaccessibility. I doubt if any art could triumph over the Grand Street trolley.

During the years of the Guild's ascendancy many other ardent groups were organized. The Stagers tried their hands at salvaging the American theatre and failed. So did Equity's official group, the Actors' Theatre. The New Playwrights, probably, to prove their modernism over the Provincetown's stable, took a disused garage in Commerce Street, called it stubbornly the Cherry Lane Playhouse and there with some of Mr. Otto Kahn's satirically inclined money set up the first avowedly left-wing theatre in New York. Though it had six authors whom Mr. Woollcott slyly called "the Revolting Playwrights," the little theatre had unhappily no dramatist and like all such theatres in such situations it presently passed away.

In the helter-skelter of enthusiastic saviors the theatre saw some fantastic events in the period between the end of the War and the end of the boom—ten years of the most spectacular inflation that the drama has been subjected to. Earnest actors and managers were assuring one another (and always the public) that the one essential was to return to the glorious, as they put it, days of repertory. We owed all these enchanting announcements to the visit of The Moscow Art Theatre. We owed the Moscow Art Theatre to Morris Gest, who embarked after the War upon what seemed to be a one-man educational campaign for the American Theatre. He brought Reinhardt and with the assistance of Bel Geddes converted the Century Theatre into a mediaeval cathedral as a background for a sumptuous and thickly-populated production of *The Miracle*. He brought a sophisticated, if light, influence in Balieff's Russian vaudeville, he brought the first company and the musical studio of the Moscow Art Theatre and he brought Duse.

Under such stimulation New York became theatre mad. At the height of its greatest enthusiasm the number of legitimate theatres within a couple of square miles had risen to nearly ninety. There had never been anything like it anywhere before.

In the flood of idealism the zealots were trying everything

79

but bumped their heads inevitably against the system encouraged by the commercial theatre. Walter Hampden set out to give the country repertory and got no further than a production of Rostand's *Cyrano de Bergerac* whose popularity knocked his repertory plans into the dustbin. Eva Le Gallienne abandoned lucrative stardom on Broadway to nurse the public on Chekhov and Ibsen on Fourteenth Street and, apart from her ruinously low prices, found herself handicapped by the popularity of *The Cradle Song*. The Theatre Guild, as a gesture of concession to the current madness, attempted a quasi-repertory system and gave it up. The inattentive playgoer, pampered by long years of getting what he wanted when he wanted it, simply had no talent for what seemed to be a game of hide and seek. Though it would appear that repertory is an excellent method for developing sensitive acting companies, it obviously cannot save the theatre unless it has dramatists behind it.

Two of the important creative figures of the new theatre, Jones and O'Neill, joined one of the prophets, Kenneth MacGowan, in founding the Greenwich Village triumvirate. O'Neill was moving beyond his early stages and Jones had already made a deep impression by his scene designs for the Hopkins productions of *The Jest*, John Barrymore's *Hamlet* and Lionel Barrymore's somewhat baffling *Macbeth*. The trio produced several of O'Neill's plays and presently subsided.

As far as the Theatre Guild was concerned in the period its general influence was more important than any direct influence on American authors. Its early productions were, with few exceptions, European. Its plays came from Strindberg, Tolstoi,

80

Benevente, St. John Ervine, Ferenc Molnar, Bernard Shaw, Capek, and Ibsen and, God save the mark, A. A. Milne. Its first important native play came at the end of its fifth season when it presented Elmer Rice's greatly underrated *The Adding Machine*. It followed this a few seasons later with Sidney Howard's *They Knew What They Wanted* and John Howard Lawson's experimental and controversial *Processional*. By steadfastly ignoring O'Neill the Guild seemed to pin its faith, among American playwrights, on Sidney Howard, and produced both *Ned McCobb's Daughter* and *The Silver Cord*. The Guild had become prosperous and had moved up to an extravagant new theatre of its own, where under steady criticism for its failure to encourage native dramatists it produced in rapid succession three plays by O'Neill and three by other native authors.

The Guild got to O'Neill just in time—at a moment, in fact, when it seemed to have forgotten its experimental intentions to sit back comfortably in complacent success. *Strange Interlude* reawakened some of the old interest and clinched O'Neill's position as the country's foremost dramatist. Fortunately for the Guild it could share in his triumph.

In the twenty years of its existence the Guild has had some good seasons and some bad. Some have been financially success-ful and some failures. Badgered by a large group of subscribers it has veered to the right and then to the left; it has moved towards the box office and then away from it; it has been as clever as some of the commercial managers in manipulating the public, and against it may be charged sins of omission and commission. But its total effect has been undeniably constructive, not only in the direct stimulation of its own audience, but in lifting the general expectation of the playgoer. It not only made dramatic art its business, but it had the commercial shrewdness to make its business an art. Except for Mr. Behrman, it brought forward no native dramatist of much importance; its school of acting went quickly by the board, its repertory was makeshift and its aim especially in late years extremely unsteady.

Yet in spite of everything its historical place is secure as a dominant factor in the American theatre. For the ten post-war years it set the pace and it lifted the level even in the frankly commercial theatre. It was an exciting pace, for in these ten years the theatre heard from a group of native dramatists of widely differing abilities, but of authentic talent. It was a decade that saw the development of such men as George S. Kaufman, Philip Barry, Maxwell Anderson, Robert E. Sherwood, Paul Green, George Kelly, Marc Connolly, Behrman and Rice. The ensuing nine years added only one name to the list, the spokesman for the new-risen left-wing, Clifford Odets.

Before examining their work, it is necessary to look again at the drama's alter ego, business. That post-war decade came to a sudden and very violent end. Bereft in one stroke of the stock market, of its paying playgoers on the one hand and its financial backers on the other, the organized theatre gave final proof of its commercialism by collapsing. Gloom fell upon it. The optimists coaxed themselves to the belief that the theatre attendance would increase on the theory that in times of depres-

82

sion people seek amusement. The answer to that cheerful argument turned out to be the pertinent question "What with?"

It takes neither a grim Spartan nor a half-wit Pollyanna to see the fact that adversity was not as disastrous as it looked. When money is tight people are obliged to be cautious, and caution means discrimination and a discriminate audience is the second necessity in a theatre whose first must always be the artist. On all sides production was drastically curtailed. The theatre is at its best when it falls back on those who care for it most. It can well afford to lose those who are more easily satisfied with the movies. It can do nicely without its inattentive friends who prefer to stay at home with their ears cupped to the radio. As well in fact, as they can do without it.

But the greatest damage done to the theatre by its new competitors was not entirely the fact that they took away its customers. They began to lure away its artists almost to the point of blanket kidnapping. Actors, authors and directors set out on a new gold rush to the lotus land of the camera and the microphone. They, too, may be the American theatre for all any of us know, for they may presently solve their mechanical problems and so transmute the thing that must always be drama into a medium that we cannot guess. If that medium is television, woe betide the movies, for the stage will then be watched by a million eyes instead of hundreds. If it be the poetic drama, as Mr. MacLeish and Maxwell Anderson believe, if indeed the nation's kilocycles are to be wooed in a passionate pentameter, then the theatre may turn to all its old glories and live again even in the bombastic periods of its worst rant.

But what confronted us was not a theory but a condition. In 1929 the theatre drew in its horns and in the political and economic upheaval that followed it discovered that, as usual with horns, one was right and one was left. The theatre of the left made a quick, bold bid for public support.

Its sporadic efforts were finally consolidated in the Theatre Union which took over the Fourteenth Street Theatre where Miss LeGallienne had been engulfed in the depression and treated New York, or at least a peculiarly susceptible part of it, to the communist drama. Most of these revealed a rather naïve defect—they could convince only those who were already convinced and this is neither good politics nor good business. With one or two exceptions the plays were crude to the point of burlesque. The capitalist villains emerged as characters out of Boucicault, and Little Eva going up to heaven in the touching finale of *Uncle Tom's Cabin* presented no sweeter picture of wronged innocence than the lustry comrades sobbing over the proletariat.

But good or bad, these plays did serve to emphasize the fact that the theatre in America had reached a maturity where it could discuss anything. It is to its credit that the Theatre Union had a full and free hearing and it was their misfortune that they had no better voices for their propaganda than the rather hollow and suspicious voice of claptrap melodrama.

New blood does not always mean a successful transfusion and within its own purposes the theatre of the Left did not succeed as a unit. It did, however, give the drama a jolt.

84

Prophets of the new theatre were passing into middle age or drifting to the desuetude of the movies. Those who had been successful were becoming conservative, if not smug. Those who had failed had lapsed into the inevitable futility. Under the stress of conflicting ideas and interests the Theatre Guild gave birth to the Group Theatre and out of the somewhat miscellaneous activities of the government's theatrical relief project sprang the newest dazzler in the firmament, The Mercury and its attendant satellites. The one intellectual line that the theatre of the Left drew clearly was the line between the theatre of illusion and the theatre of actuality, the theatre of escape and the theatre of experience.

Because it was born out of this period of stress, and because it raised at once political issues in the playhouses the Federal Theatre may as well be taken up at this point. Any sort of ultimate judgment is, in current uncertainties, extremely difficult. Partisans for and against are too frequently impelled to their opinions by a general attitude towards the central government, too personally enmeshed in political personalities to free the issues from blind prejudice.

It seems true, however, that when the theatre needs endowment to live it does not deserve to live. It is, indeed, already dead. If it cannot interest a public large enough to support it, if it cannot stand on its own feet as a free institution, no amount of propping up can save it.

This is true of private as well as public endowment, but public endowment creates the further danger of censorship, and opens the theatre to all the deadening weight of bureaucratic control. Honest opponents of the Federal Theatre objected to it chiefly on this ground, and immediately upon its establishment saw their worst fears realized. Diplomatic censorship straightway fell upon the projected first issue of *The Living Newspaper* dealing with Italy's conquest of Ethiopia, and the production was cancelled because officially the United States was on friendly terms with Italy and in spite of all evasive interpretations the Federal Theatre was official. It couldn't say certain things without involving, by implication, the government that paid for saying it.

The second objection to it was based largely on its methods, and the confusion they brought to an already complicated problem. It confused matters of art with the more urgent, but strictly humane, matters of relief. This confusion offset to a great degree many of the advantages that the scheme seemed to promise. With the backing of government funds branches of the Federal Theatre were set up all over the country, and theatre workers in distress were given employment.

If actors were to be hired because they could act, that was one thing; but if they were to be hired merely because they were destitute, that was another. The project was hopelessly muddled, and caught between its genuine desire to do plays that would enlist a large public at low prices, and the official aim to help as many people as possible. The extent of this essential incongruity may be judged by the fact that at one time dramatic critics in New York were approached with the suggestion that they refrain from reviewing the Federal Theatre productions at all. The drama was to be pampered in the dark.

In view of the public importance of the matter it is only fair to give the official version of the Federal Theatre's accomplishment. In a brief foreword to several of the published plays Hallie Flanagan, national director, made this general estimate:

". . . The Federal Theatre is a pioneer theatre because it is a part of the tremendous rethinking, redreaming, and rebuilding of America. Being a part of a great nationwide work project, our actors are one, not only with the musicians playing symphonies in Federal orchestras; with writers recreating the American scene; with artists compiling from the rich and almost forgotten past "The Index of American Design"; but they are also one with thousands of men building roads and bridges and sewers; one with doctors and nurses giving clinical aid to a million destitute men, women, and children; one with workers carrying travelling libraries into desolate areas; one with scientists studying mosquito control and reforestation and swamp drainage and soil erosion.

"What has all this to do with the theatre?

"It has everything to do with the Federal Theatre. For these activities represent a new frontier in America, a frontier against disease, dirt, poverty, illiteracy, unemployment, despair, and at the same time against selfishness, special privilege, and social apathy. The struggles along this frontier are not political in any narrow sense. They would exist under any administration. Taken collectively they illustrate what William James meant when he talked about the moral equivalent of war.

"In this struggle our actors know what they are talking about. In this larger drama they are themselves protagonists."

Undeniably the government theatre has made some excellent productions, and it has also kept people working. But considering the scope of its enterprise, considering the huge financial backing it has, and considering the assistance it has had on all sides, it has had very little effect on the general situation of the theatre in the United States. Perhaps it is too early to make useful generalizations, and certainly, since we have embarked on it, the scheme deserves the benefit of the doubt, but at the present moment its one contribution to the art of the drama seems to be a sort of news digest in factual exposition called *The Living Newspaper*. This very fluent and interesting medium presents merely a historical résumé of a given subject, some large-scale problem concerning the whole country, such subjects as electric power companies, and housing.

But when the Federal Theatre confronted a real problem in the theatre, and faced one of the finest poetic dramas of the time in T. S. Eliot's *Murder in the Cathedral* its two-headed intent proved its undoing. The stage swarmed with supers in a huge production that took on the trappings of musical comedy pageantry, when plainly the austerity and deep inner conflict of a fine tragedy demanded the most scrupulous integrity. The WPA production took a subtle analysis of one man's character and rendered it in gaudy externals that destroyed its simplicity and spiritual eloquence.

The most sensational event of the Federal Theatre's career

was the simultaneous production in 23 cities over the country of a dramatization of Sinclair Lewis's anti-fascist novel, *It Can't Happen Here*. No one can say that the official theatre has failed to try nearly everything, from Gilbert and Sullivan to Shakespeare, from caravan productions on metropolitan street corners to such aesthetic jabberwocky as *Trojan Incident*. My private suspicion that the whole spectacular project has done very little to help the theatre is based on its obvious failure as art, coupled with the equally obvious truth that the value of a commodity is not necessarily its price. Even a free show may turn out to be an extravagant luxury.

From the commercial theatre came the loud objection that the government was again competing with private business at a price level private business could not hope to touch. This was true to some extent, but since the privately operated theatre had been pretty shifty in maintaining its own price standards and observing fair practices, the complaint carried less weight than it needed.

For no picture of the theatre in America would be complete without a glimpse of its box office ethics, if I may use the term sarcastically. No control so far devised has been capable of forcing the managers to play fair with their customers, with the result that the price of a ticket is determined solely by what the purchaser is willing to pay for it. If it is to a flop he may find himself given two seats for the price of one (though not on the theory, I suppose, that misery loves company) and if the show is a hit, the customer may pay two or three, or four or five times the price marked on the ticket.

This genial system of commercial brigandage is tolerated for several reasons. If the ticket brokers think there is going to be a heavy demand for seats they make an advance buy, offering the producer spot cash for so many seats in the future. Tempted by the prospect of a quick return on his financial investment the producer (not always, but usually) yields and the price of the ticket to the public then becomes what the middleman can get for it. If he is a reputable broker he may charge no more than the customary brokerage fee; if he isn't, the sky's the limit and the public pays because it is unwilling to wait and buy seats when the demand is less urgent. Even when managers (crossing their hearts, and swearing their eternal love of the playgoer) hold blocks of seats for public sale at the box office, the scalpers somehow manage to get hold of them, and the result is the same.

But the system goes on because in the economy of Broadway a hit show can stand anything, and a flop is dead anyway and it doesn't matter. This brutal state of affairs has been brought about by various influences, high rents, the fire laws which prohibit the use of space above a theatre auditorium for office purposes, and so create a heavy real estate handicap, and finally the cost of production.

This last item has increased alarmingly until, except in cases of immediate success, it is prohibitive. From an industrial standpoint the theatre is completely unionized, and the wages are set by the unions which also determine the number of men, belonging to a given union, who must be employed on a production. Thus a play with no scene change and consequently no need for stage-hands at all, is saddled with men to change the scenery; plays that have no musical score may be assigned to a theatre listed as a musical house, and so be obliged to support a number of musicians who play, or draw their salaries, whether the producer wants them or not.

From the viewpoint of the unions, designed, after all, to protect the interests of the workers, this method is supposed to guarantee a certain amount of work, and so maintain a minimum level of employment. In periods of unemployment unions are obliged to face that problem, though it would seem to an outsider that the solution would lie in making production easier and so create more jobs. It is a problem that has the theatre tied in knots most of the time and the theatre's continued existence commercially is due solely to the fact that when it has something the public wants no cost is too high. But it is obvious that this selfish procedure curtails the theatre very drastically. There ought to be room in the theatre for plays of moderate, or limited audience appeal, plays that are not designed as popular hits, and that certainly do not deserve to fail. At present there is no room for them in the grim economies of entrenched unionism on the one hand and entrenched landlords on the other. Conventional histories of the drama have, I suppose, no business discussing such matters, but there is no use in discussing a popular art when its bosses, on both sides, seem determined to make it unpopular. The drama can do without everything except the dramatist, the actor, and somebody willing to listen, to dream, to feel, and

91

to think. The instinct of all three is happily embedded too deep in the race to be destroyed by any niggling matters of cash. When they meet in action and speech on a lighted platform in three dimensions nothing else matters.

This theatre that we have at last won for ourselves is a clutter of paradoxes. It is physically smaller on a basis of territory and population than it has ever been, yet it is at the same time larger in scope; it is fettered by more ties than ever, but finally freed of its deadliest weight—the chains of mere imitation. In performance it can be immensely stimulating, and profoundly dull. As John Mason Brown put it in *Upstage* it is "helter-skelter, often despairing, but nevertheless vigorously exciting" theatre of contemporary America.

These dominant qualities stem, inevitably, from the personalities that compose it. It is Mr. Behrman's wit (and his lack of structure) it is Sidney Howard's vigor (and his lack of style) O'Neill's glum magnificence that sometimes loses its sense of proportion. It is the Philip Barry who can be as bright and shiny as a bubble—and on occasion, as empty. It is Maxwell Anderson's muscular mind trying the toe-dance steps of poetry that croons in a Cosmic Chamber of Commerce; it is Clifford Odets being profound about nothing, and eloquent about everything.

It is Bel Geddes mounting a stage with scenic miracles to mark the grave of a dramatic pauper (when he has a masterpiece in his trunk), Miss Crothers, by her wit making the obvious seem snappy, Mr. Rice, a perfectionist in poetic realism, furious when he fails at less. It is the sardonic Mr. Sher-

92

wood turning sentimental, and the sentimental Mr. Kaufman turning satiric. It is the flip of Lynn Fontanne's impudent comedy, and the tremulous grief of Miss Lord's mysterious magic. It is George Cohan and Fannie Brice; it is Al Gordon's trained dogs; it is the haven of English stars and the hunting ground of Hollywood. It is a stageful of scenery and no play, and a stageful of play and no scenery. It is Hopkins doing *What Price Glory* and *Machinal,* and Hopkins doing *Plumes in the Dust.* Its slickness can hide its incompetence; its failures often measure its success. It is great because it can do anything, and cheap because it so frequently doesn't.

It is a theatre that still sets enough store by mechanical ingenuity (remembering the nineteenth century wonders of the diorama) to be astonished by scenery and then equally astonished by the absence of it. With equal fervour it embraces its scenic wizards when they are faithful realists and when they touch the heights of the imagination. Bel Geddes won high acclaim for his *The Miracle* and the photographic accuracy of *Dead End,* yet his brilliant project for *The Divine Comedy* finds no place. The suggestive impulse of such men as Simonson, Oenslager, Mielziner, Gorelick, and Howard Bey moves alongside the literal traditions of the late Belasco, "the great wizard," as Mr. Woollcott called him, "of 1888." The sculptural beauty of Jones's scene of Moses in the promised land for *The Green Pastures* lives next door to the tawdry peep-show of a wrecked dirigible.

The mischievous but ever vigilant George Jean Nathan once compiled a tidy and damaging book called *Since Ibsen,* demon-

93

strating, with appalling evidence, that the playwrights, in spite of everything, revert to the same old tricks, fondle the same old hokum. That is, I suppose, one of the self-preservative tricks of the theatre that keep it alive.

Of the playwrights Maxwell Anderson stands, I suppose, by the seriousness of his intentions, and the consciousness of his work, next to O'Neill. Yet it seems that the qualities which make Mr. Anderson important are the ones he prizes least, and the ones he exalts are the ones that are irrelevant and forced.

His earlier prose work suggested the poet without pointing to him. His later ones have pointed without proving. His collaborations with Laurence Stallings (on *What Price Glory*) and Harold Hickerson (on that blistering protest against the Sacco-Vanzetti executions *Gods of the Lightening*) revealed a man of compassionate nature and depth of anger. He could get mad.

When he turned to the poetic drama, somewhat self-consciously, he followed tentatively in the footsteps of the Elizabethans, which happened also, as far as the American theatre was concerned, to be the fainter footsteps of Conrad and Boker. (The heroine of *Winterset* has the same name as the heroine of *Jack Cade*.) His *Valley Forge* on an American theme seemed more original, more passionate in statement, more eloquently meant. Then he embarked on what he holds is a new departure, the treatment of contemporary, and even parochial events in terms of poetic tragedy.

Apart from the question of how timely is the contemporary this excursion seems peculiarly forced and pointless. The conventions of blank verse have nothing whatever to do with it. The question is what is the most suitable, most relevant, most exact medium of expression, and leaving out of the discussion all argument over whether it is good or bad poetry (I happen to think it is pretty bad) the point becomes one of effect, and whether the artifice of the means does not overwhelm the honesty of the intention.

The problem is one of tone and scale. Assuming that Anderson's poetic expression is all that it should be, there is no reason under high Olympus why a modern, realistically observed personality should project itself in the iambic pentameters of great Cæsar. There is no reason on earth why Mio, mouthing about pomegranates under a Manhattan bridge head, shouldn't sound like himself and not like a sack-suit Hamlet off the push-carts. If Shakespeare had written *Winterset* and given life to its prose characters, he would probably have used prose to do it. If Mr. Anderson had been able to carry their prosy nature beyond the immediate exigencies of his tale, and lifted them to some high planes of good and evil, his versifying might have sounded more reasonable.

But Mr. Anderson is a good man to have in the theatre, and the theatre owes him a considerable debt. He has a poet's heart, if not his song; he is stubborn, honest, and his secure sense of the theatre will see him through.

Paul Green's rhythm is more natural, closer to a recognizable beat of life. He, too, has the militant passions of the reformer but they spring more directly out of the emotional impact and out of a simpler, and less confused feeling for dramatic statement. His anger holds the primitive power of his humor and both of them reveal the directness of an approach, unclouded by self-conscious theory.

There was a time when Mr. Howard would have stood second to O'Neill, and there was a time when his admirers would have put him first. He has a striking and vigorous talent, full of cliches now, but genuinely promising in *They Knew What They Wanted* and at its best, to my unyielding opinion, in *Lucky Sam McCarver*. Both had the merit of fresh observation; both obviously engaged the heart, as well as the mind of the author. No play he has done since has come anywhere near them in originality and concreteness. *The Silver Cord*, in which the theme of maternal domination should have developed into a drama of fine perception, was impaired by the stale characterization, and by the woodenness of the dialogue. While *Dodsworth* was an exceedingly competent dramatization of Lewis's novel, *The Ghost of Yankee Doodle* was a bad muddle, revealing the confusion of a liberal wondering why he was so confused. *Yellow Jack* was widely heralded as a new form of drama, when it was nothing more or less (in outlines) than the mediaeval chronicle adapted to the modern saints of medical science. It had merits which were obscured in production.

Robert E. Sherwood reveals a powerful sense of melodrama with an increasing talent for lifting its meaning above the plane of violent action on the stage, and making it yield more important overtones. This was especially true of *The Petrified Forest*, in which a play with a message was cloaked, with a good deal of amusement and excitement, in the lurid doings of a Western gangster. His *Idiot's Delight* had the same melodramatic excitement, but with the headlong fury of a man attacking the stupidities of war.

Philip Barry and S. N. Behrman share honors as the theatre's foremost writers of social comedy, yet they observe their bright creatures from widely different viewpoints. Both have admirable gifts of style; both write not only with wit, but humorously. Their sense of comedy springs, however, from different sources, Mr. Barry's from moral and Mr. Behrman's from political and social incongruities. They are both smart, and their plays have the scintillant urbanity of society with the Sunday Supplement's capital S. Mr. Barry is more expert as a craftsman, while Mr. Behrman frequently confuses the point of what he is saying by the dramatic methods he uses to say it.

If the gentlemen are to be paired off in this fashion the opposing team would be composed of Elmer Rice and Clifford Odets, whose dramatic interests lie at the other end of the scale. Rice's *Street Scene* remains one of the outstanding contributions to the realistic theatre, a detailed, yet highly selective portrait of the brown-stone ugliness of a metropolitan street, a huge house sprawled across the stage, a real sidewalk for the clink of summer skaters, and its window ledges bulging with the gossipy bulk of the modern cliff dweller. Yet beyond this superficial literalness he caught an extraordinary feeling—the tragical sense of humanity outlasted by its physical properties, and the large indifference of a world, as of a house, in which people moved in and out—with a few minor decorations. His *The*

Adding Machine, a sharp, bitter and neglected play, was one of the Theatre Guild's best productions.

Odets gives the impression of putting a good deal of emotion into his plays without any real feeling. There is some rationalization towards the Left, but the method in general seems derivative notably from Chekhov. What gives Odets special place is his undeniable ability to write dialogue. It is not all good. Now and then it lapses into dreary and self-conscious postures. But when it is at its best it has a limberness, a strength, and a swiftness of movement in advancing the action, and a color that has few rivals in the American theatre. The pity is that Mr. Odets seems unable to tell when he is using what seems to be a natural gift on a theme that's worth writing or a pretentious piece of whiffle, *à gauche.*

In the detached observation and humorous statement of characters no one in the modern theatre has bettered the work of George Kelly. *The Show Off, Daisy Mayme, The Torch-Bearers* and *Craig's Wife* all revealed a sensitive, highly observant mind working on characters that were typically American, typical of the time, and truthfully set down. They are admirable examples of satiric humor, hilarious in their impact in the theatre, and devastating in their criticism.

Though he seldom stands alone on the stage, George S. Kaufman belongs in a class by himself. He works almost invariably with a collaborator, yet the traces of his work are so evident that the pieces make a picture of a whole. He is the most expert craftsman of the lot, a man wise in the ways of the theatre, cynical in his cast of mind, and hilariously caustic in his statement. His trademark is in the sarcasm of his dialogue and the slickness of his technique. He has been too much of a casual workman to get the full credit his talents deserve, and too versatile not only in various forms of writing, but in directing, to win his proper place as a dramatist. But by all the piecemeal brilliance his position is assured as one of the outstanding figures in the theatre.

One thing may be noted about most of this writing talent. It is journalistic, and it is a trait which, curiously enough, goes through the American theatre from the earliest days of the newspapers to the present.

Its effect on playwrighting in America is apparent, I think, not only in the themes but in the method of handling them. Too much of the play material is at second hand—for the most part out of the stuff of the newspaper, instead of the stuff of life. But the plays take on, as compensation, some of the immediacy and vividness of journalism. The risk is that in following the news, whether in theme or method, the drama runs the same risk that a newspaper runs, and nothing is as dead as yesterday's paper.

Doubtless, too, the movies and the radio have encouraged the theatre in this course. Its native tendency to get plays hot off the griddle has been aggravated by two media of entertainment which are frankly journalistic. With few exceptions our leading dramatists lack detachment; they are too close to the idea of the front-page headline and the best seller.

The drama, of course, needs no such newsiness. Unlike all other writing done by the human race, it is the everlasting

99

present. That is its greatness; that is its special genius. It speaks not of what happened, but of what is happening. You see it as it happens. Call it escape, illusion, or an experience in art, it is time made stationary on a separate calendar, man's temporal measure of himself. By it a country may see its own image. In a new country this may be a useful and a heartening sight.

THE
MOTION PICTURE
IN AMERICA

A HISTORY IN THE MAKING

By

RENÉ FÜLÖP-MILLER

THE BUTCHER, THE BAKER, THE CANDLESTICK MAKER...

CHAPTER I

THE BUTCHER, THE BAKER, THE CANDLESTICK MAKER...

THE CLOTHING MERCHANT, CARL LAEMMLE, of Oshkosh, Wisconsin, had counted pennies for twenty years, until he had saved enough to become independent. Then the young Swabian who had first emigrated to America with fifty dollars in his pocket, worked as errand boy for a druggist and finally graduated to the position of manager of a clothing concern, decided to go to Chicago and open his own store.

While looking for a suitable location, he chanced by a doorway before which a crowd was impatiently waiting. When he came closer he saw that he was in front of one of the new kinetoscope booths which were springing up everywhere at that time.

Laemmle stood there fascinated, watching the throng of visitors ceaselessly shoving their ten-cent pieces through the ticket window and passing inside. No sooner had one group been admitted than another formed outside.

The clothing salesman from Oshkosh had never seen such a press of customers, and he began to count the receipts. He counted until late in the evening. Next day, early, he was at the same spot counting again.

He asked the proprietor about the installation and overhead of such a kinetoscope show, and when he learned how much would have to be laid out for the projection machine, the rent of films, personnel and general overhead he calculated that this incredible popular amusement brought its proprietor in a month as much as he had been able to scrape together in all those years. That day the clothing salesman Carl Laemmle forsook the calling that had occupied him for twenty years. He invested his savings in a kinetoscope booth, and after a few months he owned two of them, then three and finally four.

The fur dealer Adolph Zukor from Chicago had loaned three thousand dollars to a friend who had invested the sum in a penny arcade. When Zukor learned that this venture was not going well he became worried, and though the fur business was profitable, he was not inclined to accept easily the threatened loss of this considerable sum; so the Hungarian immigrant, who had been first an upholsterer's apprentice, then a dish-washer and cutter before toiling wearily upwards to great respect for hard-earned money, decided to give his friend's business a once-over and thereby save his endangered loan. Zukor traveled to New York, and when he got there he had a chance to observe the tremendous appeal of the new projection apparatus. The penny arcade was transformed into a Kinetoscope Theatre. Soon not only the three thousand dollars were saved, but Zukor realized that this business not only brought in higher returns but offered greater future possibilities than the fur business, and he too went over to the picture business for once and all.

One evening after business hours the glove salesman, Samuel Goldfish, decided to sacrifice ten cents and an idle half hour and visit a little kino booth on Broadway. For many years Goldfish had worked hard in the shop of a glove manufacturer before being promoted to the position of traveling salesman for the firm; in this new capacity he visited the Far West, which was new territory for this business. By now his income had reached fifteen thousand dollars a year, so that this young man of thirty had every reason to be content with the course of his life.

Yet as he was leaving the little Broadway picture house he suddenly realized that in the future he would sell no more gloves: an entirely new career had opened up to him within the last half hour.

"Do you want to make a fortune?" he asked his brother-in-law, Lasky, that same evening, and when the latter laughingly said "yes" he proposed that they start a film company.

"A fine pair we'd make in that business," objected Lasky as

107

Goldfish developed his ideas. "I, a vaudeville man and you a glove salesman! What do we know about the thing?"

Jesse Lasky had already tried several roads to wealth and had known great success as well as sudden catastrophe. He had blown a horn in a San Francisco theatre, served as accompanist to an Hawaiian orchestra, been a newspaper reporter, dug for gold in Alaska, had been manager for the magician Leon Hermann ("the Napoleon of Necromancy"), had made a fortune and then lost most of it when he tried to transplant the Paris "Folies Bergère" to New York. Now he ran a vaudeville agency, and it was not long before his brother-in-law had once more fanned the flame of enterprise in him. Finally he declared that he would join Goldfish (who shortly thereafterwards began calling himself Goldwyn) in starting a film factory.

The new industry drew enterprising men from all walks of life, and many of the poor immigrants from eastern Europe who had come to America saw the great chance that lay in the motion picture business.

There were the brothers Schenck from Russian Poland, who had risen from the New York ghetto to the proprietorship of an amusement park; there was the Hungarian immigrant, William Fox (originally Fuchs); there were the four Warners who, inspired by the sight of thickly crowded kinetoscope performances, left their soda-water stand, their shoe-repair shop, their bicycle-renting business, to tour the small towns of Pennsylvania with their cheaply acquired projection apparatus.

Within a short time there sprang from the modest kinetoscope booths whole chains of great theatres, and great distribution and production concerns were organized. Film studios were established, stars discovered and movie palaces erected; whether the picture was short or long, funny or moving, simple and realistic, or pompous and romantic, whether cowboys shot each other or true-hearted peasants imitated the passion of Christ, it was certain—for the box-office was an infallible gage—that regardless of the sort of production, subjects, or presentation, the capital invested would bring in handsome profits.

Now the creators of this great new industry formed the youngest stratum of American society, that "second immigration," which since the eighties had brought untold numbers of poor immigrants from eastern Europe to the New World. These new arrivals could not go out into the forests like the pioneers of the "first immigration" and wring prosperity from the virgin soil. The last free land had been occupied before their arrival; now only the cities, where success was expressed simply in terms of money, were left for them. They were, thus, obliged to classify and busy themselves as members of capitalistic society, through no matter what activity. The main object was to earn money, as much and as soon as possible; for them the new homeland was nothing but a great market with offers and demands, with win-or-lose chances whose correct utilization alone could bring them to their goal.

In this world where, in place of the possession of land, homesteads and cattle herds, there was the more calculably tangible, clear profit, the goods which were to be bought or sold lost all significance for the entrepreneur. The important thing was the profit to be made from them. Once there was profit in bicycles or soda-water bottles, later in penny arcades and film booths. Depending on the psychology of the moment, the profession, the interest, and the creation were changed; one no longer worked for the thing itself, but only for the cash profit.

The greatest factor in this regard is the right instinct for the greatest needs of the public at the moment, and those immigrants from Swabia, Hungary and Poland possessed this instinct. Chance may have made them work as errand boys, glove salesmen and suit clerks, but they remained in these capacities only until their flair told them that the public longed for entertainment more than these useful articles and that this desire was becoming more and more the strongest need of America and, consequently, offered the greatest possibilities for immediate profits.

For a long time the old puritanical code of living in the United States that branded every sort of pleasure as sinful, reduced the business profits in the entertainment field, but in the last decades the spiritual inbreeding of puritanism has been broken by the influx of other more pleasure-loving, light-hearted races. The released hunger of this boundless country for entertainment and uplift could no longer be appeased merely by the customary pleasures of family parties and occasional offerings of circus and theatre troupes. There was at the same time an increase of leisure, with its accompanying increase of boredom, which according to Schopenhauer "truly is a greater calamity for humankind than hunger."

Meanwhile, engineers and chemists in laboratories had assembled an apparatus which projected moved pictures on a screen. But it took that faithful instinct for mass needs, markets and business cycles, such as only shopkeepers possess, to grasp the importance of this discovery as a means for satisfying the universal longing for pastime.

Though Edison himself would not at first believe in the commercial future of his kinetoscope, these men left all other activities in the lurch and seized upon this extraordinary machine which made it possible to take entertainment rolled up in strips, like canned meat in tins, and ship it to the most distant settlements. The moving picture engenders the pleasure that comes of manufacturable goods and permits the industrial satisfaction of spiritual needs, just as formerly the great needs for food and clothing were satisfied through manufactured goods.

Statistics show that at the present time every sixth American visits the moving pictures daily, and that a successful picture which goes all over the world is seen by twenty million people a day. From the little show booths that once were set up in the back streets of foreign quarters have arisen vast theatrical organizations whose skyscrapers border one of New York's most important squares.

In a livery stable rented for about a hundred dollars a week the first operators and actors began to work in Hollywood, using rented theatre scenery. Since then Hollywood has become the world-renowned film metropolis which harbors some sixty great studios. The twenty leading film companies employ, in production alone, 75,000 people. In the film produced by them yearly there is more fine silver than in the entire silver-money circulation of the United States. Capital invested in pictures runs to billions of dollars; often one film may cost two million. Those men who gave up their clothing firms, fur and glove businesses and repair shops to turn to the new entertainment industry are now at the head of great international trusts.

Carl Laemmle, who once opened a picture booth because he had counted the visitors at such a place and drawn the right conclusions from the result, rose to become head of Universal Pictures Corporation and a film city, with a population of two thousand people devoted to the film industry.

Adolph Zukor was sidetracked in order to save a doubtful loan and became the head of Famous Players Corporation and the Paramount organization, whose thirty-story palace in New York is reared on the most expensive land in the world and whose Hollywood studio, like an Acropolis, commands the entire film city.

Goldwyn, Schenck, the Warner Brothers, have all become powers; to them belong chains of hundreds of theatres in America and Europe. They decide issues over great distribution organizations and immense studios. Theirs is the fourth greatest industry in America.

BUSINESS GOES ARTISTIC

CHAPTER II

BUSINESS GOES ARTISTIC

IF THE IMMENSE SUMS INVESTED IN PRODUC-
tion, distribution and exhibition are to yield a profit the films
must sell to a public of millions and must suit the taste as well
as the intelligence of people in St. Louis, Buffalo, Shanghai,
Capetown and Sofia. For, any goods calculated on mass sale
must have the approval of the great masses. Therefore, the
establishment of a mean of attraction which will draw people
all over the world is the rule governing production.

The motion picture public is very difficult to define. It is a

115

varied multiplicity of races, nations, speeches and classes with the most different individualities, needs, tastes and prejudices. In its beginnings the motion picture appealed predominately to the immigrants in the harbor cities, who did not speak the language of the country, did not possess the means to have theatres in their own tongue, and who consequently had little opportunity to enjoy themselves in their leisure time. Soon, however, the powerfully growing industry was obliged to win the American countryside as a market, the countless little towns of the Middle West whose Babbitts formerly felt only an unattainable desire for entertainment. The farmers and cowboys of the little prairie settlements were there also to be converted into movie-goers, as well as the inhabitants of the big cities who by and large had not yet become accustomed to reading books and engaging in other mental activity, and who consequently needed an accessible pastime. Finally the moment came when the American film industry stretched its tentacles to foreign countries, conquering the once overspreading Europe, and penetrating even to the remotest colonies. In so far as its market encompassed the whole world from Yokohama to Budapest and from Stockholm to Buenos Aires, ignoring no human settlement, its production had to meet the tastes of the most distant peoples, the most foreign civilizations.

This was a very difficult problem, for, in addition to all the differences of race, age, temperament which nature had created in these countless individuals who had to be won to pictures, there was to be considered the multiplication of dispositions, preferences, inclinations, wishes and fears which prevented one

116

young girl from resembling another, one cholera victim a second.

The producers of other manufactured goods had an easier time, for if the size, head shapes and feet of their customers displayed great individual differences, it had been possible for, say, the clothing industry long ago to reduce these varieties to a few types. For the millions of head shapes, shoulder breadths and foot sizes there were general numbers which could serve as bases for their manufacture.

But with moving pictures the question was one of finding a common denominator for the wishes, feelings, temperaments and philosophies of life of all mankind, and also, if possible, to satisfy the spiritual needs with a standardized article which would not only be manufacturable but which would also offer each customer something that suited him.

Induced always by the greatest possible sales, these dealers developed a remarkable diligence for studying the minds of the masses, an admirable exactitude and objectivity. They arrived at an insight into the public demand for entertainment that surpassed anything commercial psychology in that field had achieved up to the time.

In this they were offered the most valuable assistance by actors, directors and authors of films, who, in multitudes, like their employers, were recruited from the most varied livelihoods. Artists and *chansonniers* from the varieties, clowns and comedians from vaudeville, waiters, street-car conductors, book salesmen and unemployed supernumeraries were drawn to the films through the same flair that had led the producers hither—

the certain knowledge that here more money was to be made than in their former occupations.

Inasmuch as the practicing artists were working to establish the motion pictures for purely business reasons, sooner or later they made the premises of their employers their own. Their task also was to please the largest number of spectators. This venal desire on the part of the performer, unhampered by any cultural background, was what really enabled the producers to guide the industry to its present commercial success.

Intimately bound to the needs, hopes and longings of the masses, these first film actors, directors and assistants acquired the sure instinct as to what the crowd must be offered in order to hold it and to evoke its tears of sorrow or laughter.

If, as Henri Bergson thinks, the film today has brought forth important artistic expression for our time, it is also true that these worthy achievements have been inspired by commercial considerations. The striving to make money has not only produced the mediocre goods of the film industry but also those forms which today offer new stimuli to literature and have found high recognition in aesthetic criticism. The greatest film artists themselves have sought from the very beginning to improve their means of expression by a constantly refined attuning to the wishes of the public.

The young Canadian copper smith Michael Sinnot, who later called himself Mack Sennett, is the real founder of the American film comedy. One day, finding his calling insufficiently profitable, and being of a flexible nature as well as possessing a pleasing voice, he decided to become a singer. But his shoulders, arched by his hard work, were so broad, and his arms so unsightly, that no one would hire him because of aesthetic considerations: so he had to look about for another occupation. When he learned that one could make good money as a picture extra he applied for a job at the Biograph studio in New York. He was hired and soon after entrusted with the staging of comic film scenes. As a former copper smith, with no literary pretensions, he developed crude jokes and primitive, grotesque situations that pleased the public.

His success as a director soon provided him with the opportunity, together with two other canny business men, to found an independent film concern which he called the "Keystone Company." Now he began to specialize in comic police films, because he had long since remarked that a policeman bested on the stage was sure-fire laugh material. He concluded, therefore, that if one giddy policeman on the stage was funny, the more of them there were the funnier it would be. Finally his pictures were characterized by a regular troupe of the most ridiculous-looking clumsy policemen.

In this manner originated the famous slapstick comedy which took its name from the rubber billies used by the policemen. All sorts of people were hit over the head with these instruments, an effect that never failed to release the most uproarious laughter. The climax of these films always consisted in a heated pursuit, involving Keystone cops, children, dogs, and every manner of living creature chasing each other. The proved comic effect of the loud circus slap was also used by Mack Sennett, within the optically demonstrable means of the silent picture.

At every opportunity he made his actors throw pies at each other. When one of these landed in the face the same laughter arose that was occasioned at the circus when the slap sounded. When it was discovered that this pie-throwing awoke in all primitive spectators a lively, infantile delight in getting dirty— from that moment on, as often as possible, someone in a Keystone comedy was being smeared with eggs, dough, porridge or any other sticky stuff.

The surest comedy effects in Mack Sennett films, however, were attained by Ben Turpin, who once in a grotesque stage rôle had injured his eye muscles and thereafter was markedly cross-eyed. When Turpin noticed that the movie public perpetually laughed at this, he avoided all medical treatment and by being as cross-eyed as possible earned a great deal of money. The comedian John Bunny, because of his corpulence, his tiny penetrating eyes, and the stupid look about his mouth, aroused hilarity; in consequence he was very careful to keep his physical peculiarity unchanged, which made him a favorite with the picture fans and brought him an enormous salary.

When all these effects finally outwore their effectiveness, Mack Sennett devised the institution of the "Bathing Beauties;" for he very correctly saw how this must fascinate the repressed erotic curiosity of the mob. He therefore organized a troupe of beautiful well-developed young ladies, and in all the following films had them appear in bathing costume. Before long these bathing beauties achieved world fame, and their pictures were spread about the earth on millions of postcards.

One of the most notable colleagues of Mack Sennett, who

contributed much to the development of the American film comedy and its characteristic style, was an erstwhile waiter named Lehrman. This latter had worked for some time in New York as a street-car conductor, and as such had traveled up and down Fourteenth Street where the Biograph Studio was located. From passengers he learned that in this studio it was easy to make a lot of money. As a result one day he gave up his job as conductor and offered his services to the Biograph Company. Lehrman later became the creator of the "gag" technique: the contriving of comic situations producing the most hilarious effects, now a well paid position in the motion picture business. This "gag" science, founded by Lehrman, soon became the basis of the comic film.

MAKING SILK PURSES OUT OF SOWS' EARS

CHAPTER III

MAKING SILK PURSES OUT OF SOWS' EARS

FROM SIMILAR SMALL BEGINNINGS, OVER A course of circumstances and considerations, was developed the career of that film actor whose far-reaching artistic significance can scarcely be denied anywhere today.

Once when Mack Sennett was in a vaudeville theatre he was struck by the ability of a young man in one of the lesser acts, a young man whose comical, outsize trousers charmed him to laughter. Some time later Sennett needed an actor and he telegraphed his representative in New York: "Find me an actor by the name of Chapman or Chamberlain or something like that, playing bits."

The agent had trouble enough locating such a vaguely defined personality; but at last, in a little town in Pennsylvania, he found a certain Charlie Chaplin, who was apparently the man he was looking for. At that time Chaplin was earning fifty dollars a week in vaudeville, yet he hesitated when the Sennett agent offered him a hundred a week. He felt that in vaudeville he had a sure job, and therefore did not wish to take a risk. It was not until the offer was increased to a hundred and twenty-five that he decided to go into pictures.

Chaplin had spent his childhood in London in the most extreme poverty. As a youngster he was obliged to earn money at part-time work in a toy factory. Often, to the annoyance of his mother, he would amuse himself by imitating a poor old man who used to hang around a London pub and hold horses for the coachman.

When he was eight years old he decided to become an acrobat and joined the Risley troupe in Middleborough. Once, while practicing the double sommersault, he fell on the upstretched feet of his partner and had the misfortune to break a thumb, which put an end to his career as an acrobat. Then he became a child dancer and finally a circus clown. An opportunity that was offered decided him to take up the career of Variety comedian. From then on he appeared in little sketches as a thief, billiard player, drunken roisterer, boxer or magician.

His film career began when Mack Sennett placed him in

his police troupe; there he tried to use those effects which had brought him success in his earlier variety rôles, but it soon became apparent that these would not produce the same results in pictures.

"It was days and days," Mack Sennett relates, "before Charlie finally produced something he could use. He tried all sorts of make-ups—one of them, as I recall, was that of a fat man—and they were all about equally ineffectual. This was so annoying, in fact, that I was beginning to feel a little anxiety as to whether my discovery had really been so very lucky."

In the constant search for new ideas Chaplin finally hit upon the type of the poor devil who through his inner superiority finally wins out against all the obstacles of destiny and withal remains still one of the people.

He himself tells the ideas that led him to develop this figure:

"A tramp in a fine hotel—that is a universally effective situation. Almost everyone has seen himself in the rôle of a poor lonely creature in the midst of a gay throng, with no point of contact and yet forced somehow to identify himself with the atmosphere about him. So I buried myself in the tiny nuances of such a figure; I practiced pulling down my shabby cuffs, getting the correct angle of the hat, all the gestures which could give the characterization a broader significance."

Soon Sennett was unable to resist the offers of competitors and so Chaplin went over to the Essanay Company. But there also he did not remain for long. Essanay tried to shut him out from any contact with the outside world, but an agent for a rival firm, dressed as an extra, managed to get on to the Essanay lot and made Chaplin a better offer. The income of the now world-famous comedian went to six hundred thousand dollars a year, then to a million. Later Chaplin decided to make his own productions, which must have brought him in even more than that.

Meanwhile, his name had achieved such popularity that in a New York show window a pair of old shoes was displayed with the sign: "These historic shoes were once the possession of Charlie Chaplin and are insured for ten thousand dollars."

The rise of Harold Lloyd also shows plainly that he achieved his success by closely studying the public's reactions. As a young unemployed extra Lloyd had one time gotten a job through a trick. In make-up and costume he had mingled with a crowd of extras outside the studio and as the throng pressed through the gate had smuggled himself in. It was only after many experiments that he too created a typical figure which soon became popular. He hit upon the idea of wearing horn-rimmed glasses (which were even then becoming an identification for American youth) for comic effect. These combined with his sometimes self-contented smile, sometimes worried face, produced the desired effect.

Lloyd himself explains his method of choosing picture subjects: "One afternoon in a street in Los Angeles I saw Bill Strothers, 'the human spider,' climbing up the wall of a high office building. The higher he climbed the more nervous I became, and when twelve flights up he had to overcome a difficult cornice I simply couldn't stand it any longer and had to dash around the nearest corner. I at once asked myself: 'If that sight so excited me, what effect must it have on the picture public?' The more I thought it over the better the idea pleased me."

From that time on Lloyd combined his eternal unchanging glasses with dangerous and grotesque situations to which, as he had learned, the public reacted most strongly.

Buster Keaton, the former vaudeville comedian, relates how he came to use the "dead pan" expression in pictures. He learned after painstaking observation that the strongest laugh effects could be obtained with this method.

"I have been working in pictures since I was twenty, and I have always made a point of exploring thoroughly the creation of the comic and to offer as completely as possible the comical. It used to be thought that the comedian himself must laugh in order to bring the public to laugh. Mirth was generally considered a sort of contagious disease that was passed from the laughing actor to the audience. On the basis of this conception the comedian was obliged to laugh himself into knots. I made a thorough study of how English comedians, whom I consider the most accomplished, attained their results, and gradually I penetrated their secret. It lies simply in the fact that the English comedian is always a little more serious than life itself. On the basis of this knowledge I set myself the task of remaining completely serious in any situation. I am convinced that the more solemn I was the more the public laughed."

But not only the comedy types of films owe their genesis to such speculative considerations on public taste. All other forms which are today characteristic of the American motion picture have profited by box-office indications which are the criterion always.

When William Fox was about to produce a play that had been inspired by a story of Rudyard Kipling, and at whose climax there appeared the figure of a ghostly vampire, an actress named Theodosia Goodman was brought on for this part. This woman, later known as Theda Bara, jealously concerned for her success, made use of clever publicity to make herself a figure of most abysmal depravity and occult oriental seductiveness. So sprang into being the vamp type (the demoniacal, seductive woman) which, having met with instant public approval, became a standard film rôle.

At first many producers believed that the names of celebrated actors and singers of the legitimate stage would prove a strong draw with the picture public. With this in view, Adolph Zukor and Samuel Goldwyn were willing to pay anything to obtain celebrated stage stars for their pictures. But it was soon apparent that these celebrities of the great theatre were practically unknown to the proprietors of movie houses and their patrons, and that their style meant little to these latter. Quite of their own accord the great masses, to whom the theatre and its art were foreign, chose their own stars, showing a preference to players whom they felt to be the same kind of people as they themselves were.

So it happened that while Zukor and Goldwyn were giving the public names like Sarah Bernhardt and Geraldine Farrar, there was developing the great popularity of a little girl, who in a threadbare jacket, with long curls about her shoulders,

130

and an innocent serious child's face had first come to the Biograph studios looking for work.

Little Gladys Smith had been barnstorming for five years in child parts. Then in New York she had attracted the attention of the famed Belasco and had finally decided to try her luck in moving pictures. Chance willed that Griffith, the director, was at that very moment looking for a young girl for his newest picture, and so Gladys Smith, who now calls herself Mary Pickford, got her first film engagement.

The same Mary, who had called at the Biograph studio that day without even enough money for carfare home, ten years later, together with her husband, stated to the income tax authorities that their years' income was six million dollars.

Through Mary Pickford the Gish sisters also came into pictures; these latter, also poor children, had known Gladys Smith in the theatre and had gone to visit her at the film studio. Director Griffith saw at once that these charming girls would please the public and engaged them on the spot.

D. W. Griffith, who was soon to become the artistic creator in modern American directorial technique, had himself come in contact with the film industry in scarcely less accidental fashion. An unemployed actor, he had tried book-selling and newspaper reporting. Then he heard that the moving picture companies needed ideas and were willing to pay for them. So he wrote a film scenario of *Tosca* and offered it to various producers. His scenario was turned down everywhere but he secured employment as an actor and a short time later, much against his will, he was entrusted with the supervision of a new film. Not until

131

then had he found an occasion to develop his real talent, and in a very few years he was counted the best and most gifted picture director in America.

When Samuel Goldwyn was organizing his film company he wished to secure Griffith's services. But Griffith wanted to know at once whether Goldwyn could show him a bank deposit of $300,000, and when the latter was obliged to admit that he could not, he refused to join him.

About this time Goldwyn and Lasky came across the young dramatist Cecil De Mille and offered him a weekly salary of one hundred dollars if he would become a director for the new concern. De Mille had not even seen a picture being made, and knew nothing about direction, but the hundred dollars tempted him, so he accepted the proposition. There was no occasion to regret this, for in a short time he became one of the most successful directors in the business.

One of the earliest pioneers of film art, Hobart Bosworth, had been first cabin boy, whale fisherman, boxer, wrestler and cowboy. After some years spent with a touring stock company in California he went into pictures and became actor, director and scenario writer. Eventually, he became president of his own company, which had great success with Jack London stories.

More than one famous film actress was discovered by a director or producer behind a shop counter, in a manicure shop or on the beach—because her face or legs were pretty, her movements charming, her glance seductive. In those days all a woman had to have was physical appeal to make the silent

132

screen her own and receive enthusiastic admiration and thousands of fan letters. A great supply of histrionic talent was not necessary—it was, if anything, a detriment.

Like the men who first developed the industry, motion picture subjects came from the most varied walks of life. Wherever the masses spend their time the film industry has gone busily a-learning. It has studied every possible experience whereby the idle, formless wishes and expectations of the dying imaginative impulse of the crowd can be stimulated.

Popular American melodrama taught the motion-picture people that the audience is thrilled if the gallant cowboy gets the better of the villain, if the angelic heroine comes safely through fire, kidnaping and train wrecks, and if the lovers at last go to the altar. From the successes and failures of the literary stage it was easy to see which dramatic motives and events, comedy effects and situations appealed to the great crowd and which met with no response.

The crime novel furnished no less important inspiration with its secret criminal bands, devilish blood-deeds, and breakneck chases which held hundreds of thousands of readers in breathless suspense.

Advertising also contributed toward understanding the feeling of the masses, for what appeared in the magazines was quite in accordance with the longings of civilized mankind: magnificent country houses, sleek automobiles speeding by, unblemished complexions, wonderfully fitting suits, superb evening wraps, completely equipped kitchens and happy, contented, smiling husband, wife and children.

From the tabloids, one could learn the art of putting the descriptive word into pictures. The short stories of the big circulation magazine, sensational headlines of the daily papers (train wrecks, murder, rape, robbery, smuggler chases and society scandals) called by the newsboys, all contribute to a knowledge of what the public thinks about.

The motion picture has taken unto itself everything that instinct and passion awakens, what inspires the man at the football game to break into yells of delight, what evokes laughter in the people in the street or the guests in a low dive when a man trips or a chair is taken from under someone, what makes the man who watches a street fight take sides passionately, what brings the man at the Sunday sermon to a state of pious ecstasy and plumbs a well of high and noble feelings. For picture men the nameless games of street urchins who throw dirt at each other are a subject of serious attention; so too are sensational jury trials, and the circus with its tight-rope walkers, clowns and lion tamers, and vaudeville with its strong-man acts, its comic dances, nudity and obscene jokes. They study college life, on which many a mature man looks back wistfully, and the primeval myths that are a part of the sensibilities of a whole people. *The Book of Moses* and the novels of Elinor Glyn are thumbed through thoroughly for suitable subjects.

They have studied the lines, lights and shadows of the great masters, and no less zealously have they turned to the lights, lines and shadows of tawdry postcard artists whose present-day popularity is greater than that of Rembrandt or Titian.

In the choice of a film subject, however, one must give careful attention to all social, sexual and race prejudices, to prevent violating any convention which would arouse the antagonism of the public. Not the tiniest detail may be released which might run counter to a social taboo.

In order to know public reaction down to the finest point the producers have established a special customer service in the theatres, which furnishes them with reports as to what scenes excited the customers, made them laugh, or made them yawn. From such observation has gradually been formed a mean of the spiritual state, a coefficient of probability of public taste, which has been taken into consideration in the making of later films.

If the results of all these inquiries cannot be absolutely accurate (for it is a question here of the least trustworthy material —human nature), nevertheless the producers have succeeded quickly in finding a relative constant in the primary functions of the soul, through the use of which the desired effect can be attained with approximate positiveness.

THE WISHING MACHINE

CHAPTER IV

THE WISHING MACHINE

THE MOTIVES BY WHICH ALL MEN ARE GOV-
erned—and whose treatment in pictures must meet with universal comprehension—are naturally the most primitive actions
and emotions which a Chinese coolie as well as an American
farmer feels, but which cannot find their free expression in a
civilized world.

One such primal impulse which has been suppressed from
its initial manifestation is the desire for power and its associated
desire for possession. Nature ironically provides that this in-

stinct be generally associated with physical or spiritual defects; and, of course, weak muscles, dulled senses or a retarded intellect deny it the proper manifestation. On the other hand, where nature is merciful, the relentless forces of an inimical outer world trample down the will to power, degrade it daily with parents, teachers, authorities, employers and office managers. It seems as though human society has created custom, laws and ordinances, with the single purpose of tormenting and ridiculing the power instinct.

In civilized life hardly anyone can be what he wishes to be. Hemmed in by natural laws, by a world of relentless fateful happenings and circumstances, the will to power finds itself in incessant confusion, embarrassment, restricted by a maze of rules and necessities which at no time allow a complete realization of this primal impulse.

It is in the domain of the sensual that the will to power and the instinct for possession are most deeply rooted and where the social regulation of passion opposes the most tormenting restrictions. No less suppressed also is the elementary manifestation of the yearning to rule, the universal inborn desire toward destruction and cruelty.

"Wait until we have a Linnaeus of the human species," wrote Friedrich Schiller, "who will classify men according to inner urges and instincts, Then how astonished one will be to find many whose vices have been enclosed within the tight bonds of burgeois existence and its laws, in the same category with a monstrous Borgia."

There is only one possibility of triumphing over these restrictions to the imagination and to satisfy the elementary need to broaden the individual life pattern: so long as a man may not practice in reality the instincts which are restricted by strong social taboos and is therefore condemned to suppress them, often painfully, phantasy offers him the opportunity for flight out of the narrow region of his customary existence into the freedom of fiction. Phantasy does away with the severest obligation of civilized life, the obligation for constant consideration of the world about. As reality lies permanently under the dictate of obligations, motives and effects, urgent duties and necessary consequences, so in phantasy we find in their place complete gratification freed from the responsibility which actual deeds incur. Phantasy creates a world in which neither strong obligations nor punishable consequences exist and in which the will to power, sensuality and the aggressive instinct, opposed by no obstacle, threatened by no punishment, can find satisfaction.

In the same way phantasy also frees men from their temporal and geographical restraints. To it, time is not a fixed, arbitrary factor and nothing prevents it from changing, without intermediary stages, the present into the past and future, to speed through centuries in a few moments, to compress or to stretch out the passage of time at will. Spatial boundaries are of no more consequence to phantasy than temporal ones. It makes man omnipresent and also allows him to live through a multitude of events in the most varied and exotic localities.

However, this substitution for a real but unlivable freedom is only perceivable to the few, since, in accordance with that fundamental principle of injustice which governs all creation, the enjoyment of phantasy is the privilege of a comparatively small number of choice spirits. Its true nature is withheld from the great masses.

But in this America which has set itself the goal of making, with the aid of mechanical creations, all material pleasure and ease of living accessible to the great masses and to compensate for the injustices of nature, it must follow *per se* that phantasy has also been democratized and is no longer the privilege of the elect.

The same mass production which enables even the poor to have good clothes, food and agreeable homes for little money, provides the imaginative poor man (at little expense) with the pleasure of imaginative experiences, wherein the unconcentrated, feeble, formless longings which are characteristic of the man who possesses no imaginative force or creative genius, are given a definite representation.

With the same ease as innate phantasy, mechanical phantasy also conquers the barriers of everyday life. With a few production tricks and mechanical artistic conceptions, it is possible for this new medium to break down the causal thought obstacle, to conjure up the past, to slip omnipresently from one spot to another, to make the whole multitude of human dream-pictures appear in play-form combinations before the eyes.

The film-maker knows that most people, like little children, run up against insurmountable barriers at each attempt to satisfy the will and that the feeling of helpless weakness thus created calls up an inner rebellion against the consciousness of this inferiority.

For the compensation-need thus occasioned, the film offers satisfaction, in that it causes the weak and the timorous to play for a while the rôles of brave self-confident successful adventurers.

To the impecunious, the film offers pictures of wealth and ease, which correspond exactly with their images of the longed-for world of luxury. To their longings is brought the illusion that there are no insurmountable social barriers, that the way to wealth and power is open to all. For the shopkeeper, tied to his little business, the film relieves the deadly monotony of his existence: it opens for him the whole world and enables him to enjoy the beauties of strange parts of the earth.

The film industry thus caters to the impoverished love need and the urge to display power, under which the sensualities bound by social and moral conventions suffer. To the erotic longings without the courage of the deed, to the ever active sexual curiosity, the movies offer satisfaction, in that they show to the public sitting in secure darkness beautiful men and women in erotically stimulating situations, dances, embraces and kisses.

But the film also meets those dark impulses that demand destruction of the established social order. If, in real life, education, law and threats of punishment have shoved the bolt against the activity of these instincts, the film spectator's sense of fulfillment is all the deeper when he sees fun poked at the guardians of the law, the heroine of the underworld idolized,

143

and, as occasion offers, is permitted to live the crimes of criminals. Thus, the motion picture satisfies even the most secret appetites, with no fear of consequences.

Just as any well-conducted business organization makes a creed of "service to the customer," so has the film industry offered everything to please its clients. It was essential, therefore, that the phantasy pictures displayed on the screen should correspond to the phantasy-urge of everyone, so that the satisfaction of the repressed impulses in the hearts of the spectators should take place effortlessly and agreeably in the course of the picture. All phases of the thrill, struggle, excitement, with which the striving for power and the sensual impulse are accompanied in real life are so arranged in the picture that the spectator needs only to glance at the screen to feel at a previously determined spot the right wish rise up within himself, and during a fixed time to feel the needful thrill, and in its proper moment to experience the pleasure-giving excitement.

Thus it is that the cinema spectator feels as though the hopes, deeds and conflicts of the actor were his very own, a process requiring only the slightest mental equipment, which (as modern psychology through investigations of animals, children and feeble-minded people has shown) seems to exist in the least developed brain. It is simply a case of exercising this gift, typical of every child and every savage, for recognizing similarities between a situation taken objectively and one actually experienced, and on the ground of such an analogy to "feel oneself into" the experiences of other people.

This primitive capacity for inner imitation and identifica-

144

tion makes it possible for the spectator to feel the passions, dangers and triumphs of the pictured hero as intensely as though he were himself that hero.

In order to facilitate this in every way, the film producers, with a remarkable knowledge of human nature and a clever adaptability to their customers, carefully avoided any form of expression that might be beyond the power of comprehension of the most limited intelligence. The smallest collective mass, the lowest grade of cultivation became the proving block of the understandability of the material used, according to the rule set forth by Paul Simmel that the intellect of the masses did not gravitate according to a mean between the highest and the lowest elements, but tended constantly toward the lowest. This point "on which a great number of individuals meet" must "lie very close to the level of the lowest among them, since the most elevated can descend but not every lowest can come up."

So long as the film was silent, the purely pictorial presentation guaranteed comprehensibility; the public could apperceive the optical impression on the screen without the slightest exertion or thought, and it was never necessary to understand abstract ideas or to transpose the words in the representations.

The invention of the talking picture jeopardized this universal comprehensibility, for now the audience had not only to see but must hear as well; it had to follow a spoken dialogue and gather the sense of the plot, at least in part, from this. But here also the way of salvation soon opened up. The vocabulary of the talking picture was reduced to those expressions which could be understood by the least educated man. Here, too, one had the same experience as with lyric writing for popular songs, whose success depended on keeping the verses within the confines of a conventional vocabulary of a few current words.

The plot itself, as in the silent picture, was constructed along effect-producing and non-intellectual motives. Accordingly, the film plot followed quite rudimentary themes which in their simplicity could be understood the world over, and their motives, which the action of the performers established, corresponded to the impulses of an instinct and inner life common to all men. Characters as complicated as the average normal man were not clear enough even for pictures. Only characters with one trait could be used—characters who through their very externals and through their behavior are easily recognized as being good or wicked, or likely to lose or win in the end.

Only when the mixture of good and bad traits in a figure is avoided, when all characters are simplified to an unmistakable type, is it certain that every customer can tell without effort which person is to be identified with a happy ending to emerge triumphant from the plot.

Here, too, special consideration is given to the sexual non-development of most of the spectators. The film industry knows that under the traditional social forms and the toil of monotonous mechanized work the free development of a sex life is restricted, and that, consequently, countless men never manage to emerge from the clumsy sexual wishful phantasy of puberty. They may long for feminine charm, for beautiful yielding bodies, seductive situations, or for masculine wooing and ardent embraces, but they lack the power to create their erotic images themselves; and at last they become victims to dull, vague, enervating longings which can achieve no form.

For such as these, understanding producers and directors, in common with erotic actors and actresses, established standardized forms for feminine charm—yielding bodies, seductive gestures, and powerful manly poses which would save the weak imagination the trouble of depicting for itself the objects of its desires and its imaginative behavior in enticing situations.

Immediately, every man whose unformed wish tended toward a charming, glamorous femininity knew that he could find his ideal ready-made in the pictures of a certain star, and women began to realize if they were to please such men, they must imitate that star.

Again, for those young men whose wish-phantasies were built about the modern, lively, athletic girl (from impressions received in autos, night-clubs, on the beach and golf course) the pictures of another diva offered the most advantageous combination of these elements in fulfilling the erotic dream-pictures. The vamp type again personifies what men with insufficient imagination vainly seek to conjure up when they are bursting with sexual energy, when they long for sinful seduction, or would like to plunge into the depths of sensual dissoluteness.

The film also offers ready-made dream-pictures to various feminine longings. For those who, in the society of an upright, clever business-man husband, feel the longing for an exotic

147

type of man there is the passionate latin "Sheik" type. Other specified impulses find their ideal in the sympathetic, smiling, brave, healthy sportsman; in the superlatively elegant cavalier and courtier; or in the broad-shouldered, good-humored strong man type.

However, with all these standardized erotic types, small powers of differentiation are required to make a choice between various stars. Here, too, the film industry (with its eyes ever on the inadequacies of mankind) was able to create remedies: for those whose completely undeveloped and undirected sexual imagination aims merely at the species, and those for whom the choice among several types involves too much effort, the film has taken from the musical comedy the beautiful, desirable, collective body of the chorus. Since their identical hips move in the same rhythm and twenty or thirty girls bend their bodies to the same dance-time, the spectator, in order to satisfy his sex longings, is not obliged to select any particular one of these women. He can interchange them without in the least interfering with his pleasure, so that the effort of choosing among many confusing types is minimized. The sex urge here is reduced to a simple desire for women.

To make important plot involutions even easier to understand, the motion picture uses, in addition to the standard type, the method of repetition. All conflicts and plot elements are constant and recur constantly in but slightly changed combinations. The picture people have instinctively understood the childish inner life of the masses and know how important for results is the endless repetition of the same impressions on primitive feelings.

The American film always offers the same stereotyped figures. They are the "hero;" and the "ingenue" or "leading woman," who carries the love interest of the "romance." This romance is always threatened by the "heavy" or "villain," or the feminine counterpart, the "vamp." Naturally, the "happy ending" enables the "hero" and the "ingenue" to get together at last, while the "heavy" and the "vamp" meet their just deserts.

Through constant repetition, these figures have gradually come to be recognized as conventional forms in whom the public can readily place its trust; like magic signs and symbols, these fixed forms and happenings evoke in the spectator the psychological feeling of sympathy, pity, joy, hate or scorn so necessary to properly follow the plot.

A further aid is the close-up. This concentrates the optic attention on those details of the large picture which are necessary for the understanding of the plot. Here the mechanism singles out single units from the multiplicity of impressions in such fashion that they cannot possibly be overlooked. At the same time everything disappears from the range of vision which can disturb or distract. In mystery films the close-up shows the important clues, lost papers, footprints, blood stains on trouser cuffs. The feelings of the actors are clearly indicated through the close-up of facial expression or a symptomatic movement. In the same way the erotic attention is attracted to the lines of

149

a beautiful back, the expression of a seductive pair of eyes, or the play of a sensual hand.

The film direction provides that the spectator has to make no mental effort to establish the sequence of the pictures seen. On the stage, when it is necessary to express the memory of an earlier situation, the hope of a future event, or the thoughts of a distant person, it is left for the public to image what has been described in words. The film shows all these associations in the flesh by suddenly "cutting in" at the proper place a picture of a past or future event or the absent person; consequently the film spectator does not have to make the effort of association.

Thus we see that every conceivable effort is made to enable each spectator to realize his wish-phantasy in the most effort-less and comfortable fashion, so that he has nothing to do but watch the screen in complete relaxation, freed from the eternal necessity for watchful care that real life occasions, freed from the strenuous effort of attentiveness, of the obligation to think.

The vast mass of men who have not been endowed by nature with the intellectual power to imagine for themselves their wish-phantasies are spared this exertion by the phantasy-machine which delivers them the ready-made picture as purchasable goods. It was inevitable that a discovery that could create for millions so important a joy previously denied them, should have developed into a tremendous commercial success.

THE PLOT FORMULA

CHAPTER V

THE PLOT FORMULA

THE MOTION PICTURE HAS BECOME AN AC-
cessible means of wish-fulfillment for all. But the wish is undoubtedly the clumsiest and least creative expression form of
human imagination; its field of vision seldom extends beyond
the circle of immediate everyday life. Though the urge for
boundless freedom is present in it, and the magic powers of
imagination enable it to relegate the laws of nature to temporal
and spatial distance, in the wish the divine striving for endless
display attains its pleasure mostly through the hero's securing

153

an important place in a large manufacturing concern or making a wealthy marriage. So the sovereign supremacy over space, time and causality with which imagination endows men, is employed in the service of wishful thinking only to the extent of promoting the clerk to the president's desk, of giving the factory girl the sumptuous wardrobe of the millionaire's wife.

In real life, where events occur according to the stringent laws of causality and likelihood, it is always a long time before the clerk becomes head of the firm, and he must undergo many hard trials and struggles, display many special capacities, before he can lock the president's door from the inside. Indeed, often enough, a whole life is spent behind the desk without this event ever coming to pass. And, certainly, not all factory girls are discovered, loved and married by millionaires, and very few, indeed, have the opportunity to wear ropes of pearls or to wander through marble halls.

As a matter of fact, wishful thinking is built around the exceptional case, from which it readily derives the conclusion that what has happened once can happen again. Since the wish rarely possesses the power to free itself entirely from the control of the reasonable, it ventures mostly into such representations as can be summoned up out of reality as opposed to the critical objections of a pessimistic consideration of preceding instances. Therefore, it preferably borrows its dream-pictures from the idea of "I have been there before."

In the same way the wisher borrows mainly from everyday life the villains, secondary actors, intriguers, supers, settings and props which are grouped about the victorious apotheosis of himself. He peoples the scenes wherein he triumphs over hated rivals, and achieves fame, power and wealth, with other business associates, boards of directors, managers, from his own contacts; and he builds his wish world with the vulgar façade and staircases of gaudy mansions and night clubs.

As wishful thinking borrows its scenic material principally from reality, so also in moving pictures the events are taken from the real world about. Consequently, the film, whose commercial success depends on the extent to which the public can "feel itself into" its characters and their doings, must devote careful attention to the nature and pictorial content of the wish-dream. It, therefore, avoids anything in the nature of free invention or true phantasy which could be appreciated only by spectators themselves endowed with imagination. The heroes of pictures are really not mental pictures, like the characters of fairy tales, poetry or fiction. They are chiefly nothing more than photographs of banal, everyday figures. But their destinies evolve in such fashion that the public feels them possible and desirable for themselves.

On this premise, the course of events follows not the objective law of life, but the subjective wishes of the individual. So the action of a picture usually begins in a milieu painted as true to nature as possible, with figures whom the spectator can believe to be of his own world and in whom he can easily feel himself; but from then on reality—since the greatest apparent probability would lead to a conclusion not corresponding to the optimistic wishful thinking—is imperceptibly abandoned and the film story permits itself to be completely guided by the wish.

Where life usually inflicts failure, or at best creates a compromise, the film selects the exceptional case of complete success; and where reality necessitates a weary wait of years between hope and fulfillment, the film permits its heroes to overcome all obstacles in a few hours and thereby to achieve their goals. But the film's gift of invention, like that of the wish, exhausts itself in finding the exception to the rule.

It is rare that the motion picture ventures on a truly imaginative construction of milieu or characters; it utilizes the freedom of phantasy only to the extent of combining, juxtaposing or intimating real elements in accordance with the wishes of the spectator, so that the routine technique of the "happy ending" is realized.

Most often when enterprising directors have tried to make a film end as it logically should, the public has made its disappointment known.

The film version of Tolstoi's *Anna Karenina* originally ended, like the novel, with the downfall of the heroine; but in the little towns of the Middle West this unhappy ending was so unpopular that the producers were obliged to supply *Anna Karenina* with a happy ending.

Such experiences have strengthened American producers in their conviction that the commercial advantages lie in satisfying the desire of the mob for the happy ending without reservation or contraction. It has been constantly shown that the patrons of motion pictures demand a true-to-life dénouement of the film plot, but will not tolerate a veracity carried through to a tragic end. No one wants to pay to identify himself with an unfortunate hero and have his imagination led not to the victory he desires but to the defeat he fears.

It is in the very nature of the wish-phantasy, which the film sets out to fulfill, that the feeling of a tragic-heroic union with destiny is lacking. On the contrary, man withdraws into his wishful thinking to escape the serious discussion of his destiny, so that he flees before the "will" and "must" of life into his wishes.

Instead of devoting himself in his daily work to the realization of his life goal, the wisher devotes himself to the vague expectation that the wish alone is enough to bring the thing to a happy ending.

Since wishful thinking is built outside of all experience and is undisturbed by the endless resistance of men and the decrees which oppose all success in real life, it is able to lead to an artistic happy ending. The recognition of the causal connections of every event which must rob the human race of the ancient belief in the possibility of magic, has never gained admission into the realm of the wish.

Therefore, the opponents of the hero in the film are only technical, routine inventions, so that from the first moment on it is an unequal struggle. The task of the "villain" lies merely in providing through his intrigues, cruelty and dangerous persecutions, the requisite brief excitement which paves the way for the thrill of the happy ending.

Cruel parents are there to be convinced of the worth of their daughter's poor lover so that in the final scene they may give their blessing; horrible adventures threaten the lovers just so that everything may be the happier when they have overcome them; the hero experiences fright only to the end that he may become a hero under the influence of the girl who loves him; wrong exists only to be punished; old friends quarrel only to become reconciled again; the husband is led astray by the vamp only that he may be brought back again to his humdrum but virtuous wife.

Inasmuch as the "film drama" offers wish-fulfillment instead of experiences from real life and usually avoids any true discussion of the tragic problems of life, it cannot produce true characters who gain stature and form from the very struggle with life. In their place are shown clichés, and in the place of the rich variations of real life the spectator is offered the unvarying form of the "happy ending."

THE COMEDY DRAMA

CHAPTER VI

THE COMEDY DRAMA

LIKE ALL OTHER FORMS OF THE FILM, THE comic film also aims at creating for men the feeling of escape from the pressure of hard reality. But whereas in other films this takes place only at the end after the conquest of active obstacles, the film comedy, from the very beginning, places the spectator in an atmosphere of mirthful elevation above the disagreeableness of actual life. Since the comic film displays in its very form the superiority of man over the world, and since this type of film does not require the customary process of wish-

161

fulfillment, it is not slavishly bound in its choice of expressive material to the truly natural as is the case with the wish-fulfillment film. Whereas the latter must derive its credibility from a semblance to reality (so that the spectator can feel himself part of the plot and identify himself with the heroes), the comic film needs no such identification. It can start with the premise that it is all in fun, and thus it enjoys the freedom of play which allows it to form its characters according to a higher and more artistic verity.

So it happens that the mob which would never allow itself to recall in the movie theatre the true difficulties and conflicts of the world about, greets enthusiastically the stylized exaggerations of these elements so inimical to mankind. This implies an understanding of "jest situation," one of man's earliest excitements. Even the infant, within certain limits, can distinguish between the serious and the jest action, and he reacts to the latter with expressions of joy. In this comprehension of the "not seriously intended" the child indicates for the first time a complete command of the situation, a joyful superiority.

The same effects are also produced on its public by the comic film. The moment all the elements of depressing reality are denied, the spectator feels his own superiority. This increases with the increase in obstacles, and even the painfulness of situations is overcome by the power of the comic feeling.

The serious film concerned with wish-fulfillment may bring into play only the libido and its external obstacles, but the film comedy escapes reality easily through a knowledge of a universal principle which lies behind the most varied chain of circumstances. It transcends the exposition of those restrictions which hinder human urges through social circumstances, traditional and social conventions, intrigues, plots and mischances; yet at the same time it also shows the far greater struggle which the individual must unceasingly wage against the dull enmity of the material world.

What the "film drama" would never attempt to show, the film comedy shows—but in a spirit of play: man must defend himself constantly against the malicious, inexorable mechanism underlying all appearances, a mechanism with which one can never be reconciled nor from which one can ever expect mercy, because it is built on established precedent and operates according to law.

The film commands particular equipment with which to show this mechanism of inanimate things. Its technique offers the possibility to call attention sometimes to a detail of the general event, such as a part of the body, a gesture, a tiny object, a satanic knitting together of objects, and to provide a glimpse of their fiendish, inimical, mechanics independent of human intelligence.

In the first primitive days of the American film comedy, in the "slapstick tricks" that Mack Sennett created through coarse grotesque situations, there was offered a significant insight into that principle of mechanical indolence inherent in all life activity—that principle which makes it possible to change human limbs into elastic springs, the movement commenced being carried to its stupid end automatically and thereby leading every impulse through a chain of elastic reactions to an unexpected conclusion.

The policeman of the slapstick comedies, when hit over the head, falls stark and stiff to the ground, only to bound back up again like a roly-poly. The man hurled from a window hits the ground and bounces back to his starting point; the man who has had the chair pulled from under him and completes his sitting-down movement on the floor; the fist that fails to reach its objective and carries its possessor around in a helpless circle; the rushing oncomer who collides with a lady who spills her cup of tea on an old gentleman who falls back in a window which falls on the head of the policeman standing underneath.

If these slapstick burlesques showed such mechanical reactions merely to be phenomena resulting in comic effects, modern film-comedy technique invokes the same principle by making a living man the hero who must overcome these blind reactions, who must struggle against the inherent maliciousness of things. Thus, the film comedy becomes a practicable, real expression of a fundamental life conflict and, consequently —art. Every triumph that Harold Lloyd or Laurel and Hardy achieve over the outer world, is more than the cheap victory of wish-fulfillment over merely fictitious obstacles; it is always a victory of the mind over the dead mechanics of the Thing, a victory of the higher life principle over the lower. No matter how devilish a knot of conflict the material elements may entangle themselves in, Harold Lloyd outsmarts them by spontaneous ideas, intelligence, invention. When all means of communication may conspire to prevent him from reaching his job, he pretends to be the victim of an accident and uses the ambulance for transportation; thus the inimical conspirations. When the brutal, soulless strength of the strong man presses the unarmed Harold against the side of a ship and tries to brain him with a bludgeon, Harold immediately discovers an iron belaying-pin that wards off the blows and makes the uncouth brute retreat with a broken stick.

As Lloyd shows himself superior to every situation, so Chaplin displays an eternal superiority to life. If the triumph of the former is achieved through discipline, sudden inspiration, presence of mind or cunning, in his case it is by nobility, by the entirely spiritual bearing of the hero.

The film figure of Charlie Chaplin is that of the man delivered up defenseless to all the meannesses of destiny—the man who has nothing to oppose to the blows of life except an inner strength of soul. When he does not achieve that for which he longs he at least knows how to resign himself worthily, and the little gestures of renunciation, which form the end of practically all these tragi-comedies, permit him to conquer in a higher sense, when opposing circumstances have apparently downed him. He renounces and goes on his way with courage undaunted ready to try his luck in another battle some other time.

When the ragged tramp takes off his fingerless gloves in order to select the right end of a cigarette from the old sardine box that serves as a case, his movements have a nobility which is in no wise affected by the poverty of outward circumstances. And at the meager meal to which he has invited his New Year's

165

guests, the freezing gold seeker knows how to set the table so charmingly that each of the visitors feels that the dignity of the house depends not on the things in it but upon the master.

This removal of the victory from the material to the intellectual sphere constitutes a substantial refining in the film. Even more significant, however, in Chaplin's work is the fact that the realm of inimical powers is no longer restricted to the outside world but reaches deep into the man himself. Chaplin shows how the mind has not only to be on the defensive against objects outside of self, but how much more the evil mechanism in the body constantly strives to deride the mind, to defame its dignity, and cause every exalted beginning to be wrecked by physical insufficiencies.

While the soul freely and easily roams from one situation to another, the indolent body drags ill-naturedly and protestingly behind. To the moral personality it opposes the stupid indolence of its mechanistic materiality which makes it continue along the lines of acquired habit.

Charlie gets in a scuffle in a music-room and his mind is stirred by memories of esthetic pleasure; but his body is pinned under the other fighters, so he kicks his hated adversary (on the other side of the curtain) while his eyes express the deepest emotion.

Of what use to the now wealthy Charlie are the costly furs and a pocket full of bank-notes? His body still contains his former poverty when it forces him through long habit to stoop and pick up the butt on the ground. What the front confirms the back denies. The spiritual principle is always mocked, disavowed, demeaned by the mechanistic of the body.

Chaplin's films demonstrate clearly that only a very small part of the individual is spiritual. It is a tiny divine spark that fights against the material in the body and round about the body.

But this very knowledge with which Chaplin constantly provides us, allows us to grasp the whole heroism of mankind, for in the last analysis the tiny spark is the victor over the cruel, crushing mechanical entity which lies beneath all materiality.

TECHNICAL DEVELOPMENTS

CHAPTER VII

TECHNICAL DEVELOPMENTS

THUS THE FORM OF THE COMIC FILM GIVES free rein to the imagination and provides the possibility for many artistic constructions. But in the other varieties of film production, constant attempts at the artistic also have been made, despite the numerous arbitrary conventions, the stifling necessity for type-ing and the formal "happy ending." In this connection we should mention, alongside the Europeans Jacques Feyder, Korda, Lubitsch, Stroheim, Stein, Sternberg and Viertel, certain American directors, above all Griffith,

171

Cecil de Mille and King Vidor; and actors such as John and Lionel Barrymore, Chaney, Douglas Fairbanks, Senior, Laughton or Boyer, and actresses like Garbo, the Gishes, Bennett and Talmadge, Colleen Moore, Mary Pickford, Norma Shearer, Gloria Swanson, Claudette Colbert, Margaret Sullavan, Katherine Hepburn and many others.

Even the executive and technical heads of the film industry are not apathetic to the artistic problems of motion pictures. The systematic research of the Academy of Motion Picture Arts and Sciences in Hollywood has provided many important contributions to the clarifying of the esthetic side of film production. Following the same direction, the University of Southern California established courses with discussions on film art, with participation by such producers as the late Irving Thalberg, Commodore St. J. Blackton and especially the late Paul Bern, whose skill made him the acknowledged leader in all artistic and mass-psychology problems.

Such investigations and discussions have shown only too clearly how many obstacles stand in the way of a free artistic development of the motion picture. The greatest hindrance to a full artistic fruition has proved to be the obligation to imitate nature which has been imposed by public taste.

Friedrich Schiller once defined the relation between reality and its artistic reflection thus: the reflection is only esthetic "so long as it is sincere and expressly renounces all claims to reality, and so long as it is independent and lacking all assistance from reality."

"The moment the reflection is false," Schiller continues,

"and simulates reality, and as soon as it is impure and requires nature for its effect, it is nothing more than a low tool for material aims, and is no proof of the freedom of the mind."

It is characteristic of all great works of art that they are completely independent of the physical reality of their subjects, thus demonstrating clearly the principle that the outer formalization and invention of art never disturb the inner reality. The work of art, in order to be credible, does not need any identification marks of petty verisimilitude, since it possesses that deeper truth which lies in the artistic reflection, the symbol.

But the film must reckon with a great plurality of mentally undeveloped people who are not in the position to understand any other than an objective truth, and for whom only that passes as true which can be "really experienced." We know that children and primitive peoples follow a story with interest only so long as they can accept it as having "really happened;" so generally the tale closes with a turn in which the narrator affirms that he participated in the story as an eye-witness or that he learned about it from a trustworthy source. Like the fairy tale, the film must take this mental quality of its public into account and seek to create the impression that it is recounting real happenings.

The film, consequently, is not really free to imagine. Therefore, it can use invented situations, such as would not be possible in real life, only by means of tricks which give such details the appearance of the "actually happened." But this constitutes no problem since the simple man regards any photographic

173

illustration as an authentic, documented reconstitution of reality, whereas actual photography furnishes the most brazen falsification of reality. Buildings of canvas and paper can be so photographed that they evoke on the screen the full illusion of authenticity, and by means of countless camera angles, lighting, perspective and double-exposure the most absurd can be made believable.

In this regard the modern director has an inexhaustible repertory of tricks at his disposal, and these enable him to combine genuine shots of landscapes, cities and natural phenomena with particular scenes, and to place in the shutter of the camera painted glass miniatures in such a way that it is impossible to discern where the real scene and the painted scene overlap. He has proved for himself that with such technical adjuncts, naturalistic effects can be attained. The "Chinese street" on the lot of a Hollywood film studio produces shots of such local coloring as could never be found all combined in one spot in China itself.

The American film company gets to feel this superiority of the studio over reality. One studio even went so far as to obtain the film rights to a Mexican revolution. It is a matter of knowledge that the rebel leader, Pancho Villa, was paid $25,000 to do his best to fight the most important battles near the film operator and in the best camera light. He even undertook to provide for his American business friends by bombing a group of war-prisoners with grenades, so that one could see real bodies of men shot through the air in bits. But the effects of these pictures were not satisfactory, and the film company finally was obliged

174

to conduct the rest of the campaign in its Los Angeles studio. There it was possible, with a well-written scenario, the noted director Griffith, and highly atmospheric settings of wood and papier-maché, to fight the biggest battles, and these forged pictures evoked in a much higher degree the desired impression of genuine, bloody war horrors.

During the past few years this naturalness in film photography has been reinforced by the addition of the sound-apparatus, so that now people on the screen talk and make noises exactly as in real life. The water fowl now splashes not only optically, but acoustically as well; the stairs creak; and the gate of the castle falls in with a loud crash. The film has made additional technical progress in natural colors which further enhance the illusion. Three-dimensional films should complete the moving picture's ability to present completely deceptive replicas of nature.

These faithful imitations of reality are directly opposed to the true purposes of art which is not reproduction but production. A purely external imitation can lead only to a reproduction of the represented object but never to a new creation. Thus, we see in the film two conflicting tendencies: while the artist strives for the free activity of his imagination, the increasing trend toward the naturalistic in film technique is being constantly more restricted in the field of its development.

Many of the painters, designers and architects employed in the film industry feel this breach painfully and strive all the harder to use the technical advantages of pictures not merely to imitate reality but for an artistic stylization. If the originality

175

of their work is usually lost en route between sketches and production (because the producers demand constantly greater faithfulness to nature), nevertheless, the work of W. C. Menzies, A. Grot, A. Gruenberger, Gibbons, Urban, Usher and others clearly indicate that here the possibilities offered by the vast mobility of the film camera, by the introduction of models and miniatures, and by lighting technique are used to great advantage. These painters, designers and architects have learned to see men and things, landscapes and buildings from completely unusual visual angles, and it seems reasonable to expect their work to produce fruitful and stimulating results outside motion pictures.

In no other category of motion pictures has the artistic inspiration been able to develop so purely as in the animated cartoon film, since in this form there is complete freedom from the compulsion to imitate nature (which already distinguishes the regular comic film).

The films about Felix the Cat and Oswald the Rabbit were astonishing because of the very originality of the ideas developed therein, but Walt Disney, creator of Mickey Mouse, achieved the most significant artistic effects in the animated cartoon. And in *Snow White* he showed what could be done with a full-length picture.

Endless, painstaking, technical precision-work is necessary to assemble such a film from countless single pictures drawn with india ink on celluloid. One second of playing time alone requires twenty-four drawings.

Since nothing in such films is actually photographed, the

176

limitations of the "true to nature" ideal are completely lacking. These drawings can follow the flight of a rich imagination unhampered, and thus in the sphere of Mickey Mouse the artist can abolish all the stiff categories of the world of actual phenomena.

In protean fashion everything changes to everything else—animal into man, man into animal, non-living to living, organic to mechanistic, landscapes to humanlike countenances. Limbs shorten and lengthen phantastically; they change themselves into useful articles; the cow's teeth become a chimes; the nipples of the mother pig become an accordion; the goose's neck a trombone. Adventurous animals appear and make strange movements to strange sounds, and in their mad dance houses and mountains take part with rhythmic undulations of their contours. We have the impression of seeing the ingenious drawings of a Bosch, a Breughel or one of the great caricaturists of the nineteenth century awakened to phantastic life on the screen.

THE BATTLE AGAINST
VERISIMILITUDE

CHAPTER VIII

THE BATTLE AGAINST VERISIMILITUDE

A FEW ARTISTS, ARCHITECTS AND DESIGNERS
have attempted to combat the inclination of the screen toward
the "true to nature;" in similar fashion many directors have
learned to overcome the naturalistic tendency of speech in the
sound film and to subject this to an artistic stylization. If the
invention of the talking picture at first seemed to release an
even stronger inclination toward primitive imitation, today the
best directors are emancipating themselves from such slavish
verisimilitude and are endeavoring to develop a new form

181

of spoken expression within the limits of the sound picture.

Long before the discovery of the sound picture the well-known German author and director, Berthold Viertel, through his scenarizing of the works of Georg Kaiser, Walter Hasenclever and other modern authors of the German stage, contributed materially to the development of the new condensed-form of dialogue. Though this form may not be justified in the talking picture the method of economical expression has proven the only right one, as observation has shown. The use of fewer but more carefully chosen words, in conjunction with the optical aids of the picture itself, is sufficient to evoke in the auditor the illusion of detailed dialogue. On the basis of such knowledge, Viertel and other sensitive directors have often succeeded in achieving genuinely artistic effects in the talking film.

Among the most significant efforts in this direction are the dialogue pictures of Walter Hasenclever and the later pictures of the great Russian director Eisenstein, who in his gold-rush film made for a California company limits sound to noises, interjections and, at especially dramatic moments, a word or cry. In *Thunder over Mexico* he used only sound effects.

In evaluating the achievements of artists and designers, one must not overlook the great difficulties and restrictions with which they have had to contend. Occasionally, the producers may consent to artistic experiments, but they know that a preponderance of such tendencies might jeopardize the commercial success of their product and therefore must be prevented. They can subjugate the most stubborn spirits to the box-office reports.

It is a general working principle in the studio that individual artistic ambitions must not cause any real commercial damage. All important decisions as to the sort of production and the peculiarities of the piece are submitted to a fairly large collective group, the majority of which represent the commercial interests.

Writers are required only to do stories. Everything else is done by departments of especially schooled specialists. Thus, almost every picture that comes from the great Hollywood studios is a collective product in whose execution a great number of people have taken part.

In the same way the free inspiration of the actor is carefully restrained. The director gives him the most meticulous directions for each gesture, each facial expression, each word spoken. The degree of natural verisimilitude in designs is carefully prescribed for the designers and artists, and their work is checked by specialists for the most complete physical correctness. The board of executives consisting of the production director, his under directors and supervisors watches to see that each detail of the film in production corresponds to the current wishes of the masses.

While the picture is still in production, those reels of film that have been shot are sent to the projection-room and anything which the executive board decides will not be effective with the public is cut, rewritten, redirected and retaken. Regardless of protests from the authors, actors, artists and directors, the board arbitrarily changes the construction of the story and the staging, eliminates substantial parts in order to substitute others, makes the actors try new ways of feeling love, hate, joy or disappointment.

Thus, the production heads see to it that artistic experiments remain harmless episodes. From the economic standpoint this has a solid basis, for such efforts have only too often brought financial catastrophe in their wake. Even when Griffith with his film *Intolerance* undertook to show the literary idea of human intolerance, he met with a cool reception from the public, and this film produced a million-dollar deficit.

Because of this constant preoccupation of the film industry to avoid at any price anything that the mass intelligence may not comprehend, it has robbed the film of the possibility of developing a genuine artistic form.

When Samuel Goldwyn once sought Bernard Shaw's coöperation in the creation of a "truly artistic film," Shaw reminded him wittily of the misunderstanding which underlies the literary ambitions of the producers.

"We do not understand each other, Mr. Goldwyn," said the Irish playwright. "You are talking of art—I'm talking about money."

THE FUTURE

CHAPTER IX

THE FUTURE

IF THE FILM CAN BE SPOKEN OF AS AN ART FORM only with reservations, it should not be forgotten in the use of so strict an esthetic scale that the legitimate stage and literature also are seldom free of commercial considerations. These too have become entertainment industries—dependent on the box-office.

Looked at in this light, however, the film, through its honest creed, devotion to business, and through the consequences of its consideration of public taste, has contributed greatly to the cultural pattern of our time.

187

It is true that the motion picture has developed not through the poetic urge of artists for creation, but from the calculations of shopkeepers, with the result that the film from its earliest beginnings until the present time has been mainly inspired by the desire for profits. The demand has determined the character, themes and styles of its products; without undue artistic considerations the movie producers have dared to throw themselves completely on the instincts of the public.

Only an entertainment form whose creators are concerned with winning the approval of a public of millions, with no regard for traditional esthetic prejudices, may give us valuable material for the knowledge of what the masses wish, fear, hope, and what constitutes the reality of their inner life.

The motion picture is a marvelous index to the primary functions of the human soul, the lowest human impulses which are the same for all individualities. It wraps us up in a sort of spiritual pre-history. Yet how important this must be for the understanding of each individual, even the most highly developed individual, modern folk-psychology has taught us. Many of those primitive impulses and universal images are effective in the subtlest expressions of the personality, and the pre-logical element of the mind is never quite lost in the constantly advancing intellect. Yet there is no individual who has not a typical standard; no spirit, no matter how independent, that is not bound to the human society with a thousand bonds, so that he could be taken as representative of a general type.

He who would really understand and judge the intellectual achievements of mankind must carefully observe also the uni-

188

versal and lowest primary functions. August Comte enunciated this very idea when he said that man may not know mankind merely through men, and that, on the contrary, man must seek to understand men through mankind.

PHOTOGRAPHIC SECTION

THE
AMERICAN THEATRE

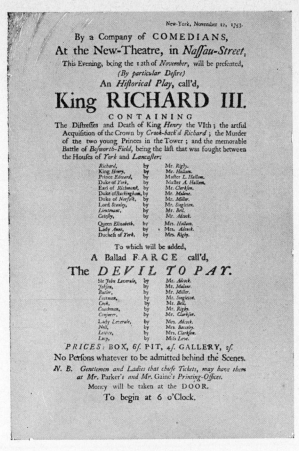

Theatre program of 1753

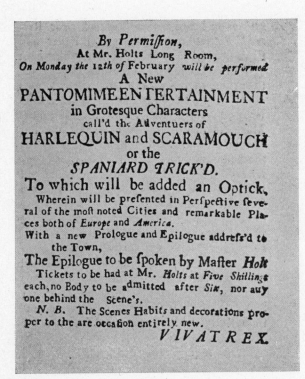

1739 theatre poster

1767 theatre announcement of the Hallam troupe

John Street Theatre, New York
(from Odell's *Annals of the New York Stage*)

John Street Theatre (*Theatre Arts Monthly*)

Scene from *The Fatal Wedding,* at the Grand Opera House, New York

Scene from Belasco's *Sweet Kitty Belairs,* at the Belasco Theatre, New York

Scene from the comedy *Today*, New York

Comedy scene from *The Scrubwomen's Ballet*, New York

Edwin Booth as Hamlet

Joseph Jefferson as Rip van Winkle

Clyde Fitch

Steele Mackaye

Henry Miller

William Vaughn Moody

Bronson Howard

Dion Boucicault

David Belasco (Photograph by Dr. Arnold Genthe, New York)

Louis Wolheim and William Boyd in Anderson and Stallings' *What Price Glory?*

A scene from *What Price Glory?*

William Boyd as Sergeant Quirt in *What Price Glory?*

Broadway as presented in Vienna (Photograph by Willinger, Vienna)

Chinatown Theatre in New York (Photograph by Gregor)

A scene from *Daughter of Heaven* at the Century Theatre, New York (Photograph by White)

The cast of the Viennese production of *Broadway*. The girl in the last row is Marlene Dietrich before her advent to Hollywood

A scene from the operetta *The Student Prince,* at the Shubert Theatre, New York

A garden theatre in St. Louis

Fiesta Theatre in Santa Fe

The late Prof. George Pierce Baker (Photograph by Marshall)

Cyrano de Bergerac as presented by the art students of the University of California

The University of Montana Theatre

An eighteenth-century school theatre at Lambach, Austria (Photograph by Gregor)

Scene from *The Winged Soul* by Marie Warren Potter, as presented at Wellesley College

The Passion Play, as presented at Canisius College, Buffalo, New York

Another scene from the Canisius College *Passion Play*

The natural theatre at the University of North Carolina

William Goodridge's presentation of *Anne Pedersdotter* at
Carnegie Institute of Technology

Maeterlinck's *Sister Beatrice* as presented by Lester Raines at the University of
Minnesota

Scene from a sketch presented by Inter-Theatre
Arts School of Acting

The wedding scene from William Sutherland's production of *The Beggar on
Horseback* at the University of Washington

Masefield's *Good Friday* as presented at
the University of Toronto

The Ohio State University Stadium, which was converted into a theatre by
H. L. Sherman

Čapek's *The Makropolous Secret* as presented by The Harvard Dramatic Club

Shakespeare's *As You Like It* as presented at the Cornish School's Theatre

Colin Campbell Clement's *The Haiduc* as presented at the Summer Theatre of the
Gloucester Players

The witches scene from *Macbeth* as presented at Stanford University by
Gordon Davis

A production of an original play by The Carolina Playmakers

Alexander Wyckoff's *The Fan* as presented at the
Carnegie Institute of Technology

Scene from *Aucassin and Nicolette* as presented by Edith L. King-Coit at the Children's
Theatre, New York

A puppet used in the Clark Puppet
Theatre's presentation of *Dr. Faustus*

The character "The Devil" in Dilley's
Puppet Theatre

The character "The Black King" in
Dilley's Puppet Theatre

The puppet character "Avarice" designed by Katherine
McEwen for *Dr. Faustus,* as presented at the Arts and
Crafts Theatre

Puppet character in *Dr. Faustus* as presented at Helen Joseph's Puppet Theatre

A scene from *Robinson Crusoe* as presented at Bobby Fulton's Puppet Theatre

A scene from *Jack and the Beanstalk* as presented at Bobby Fulton's Puppet Theatre

A scene from *A Stolen Beauty and the Great Jewel* as presented
by Tony Sarg's marionettes

A scene from *Cinderella* as presented at Dorothy Heizer's Marionette Theatre

Ellen Terry as Lady Macbeth

Mrs. Siddons as Lady Macbeth

John Barrymore (Photograph by Dr. Arnold Genthe)

Eva Le Gallienne (Photograph by Dr. Arnold Genthe)

John Barrymore as Hamlet (Photograph by Steichen)

Lillian Gaertner's design for the ceiling of the Ziegfeld Theatre, New York

Joseph Urban's design for a setting for *Parsifal*

Claire Eames
(Photograph by Dr. Arnold Genthe)

E. H. Sothern as Hamlet
(Photograph by Dr. Arnold Genthe)

Helen Gahagen (Photograph by Dr. Arnold Genthe)

227

Joseph Urban's design for the grail scene for *Parsifal*

Joseph Urban's design for a setting for *Fidelio*

Alfred Lunt and Claire Eames in *Juarez and Maximilian* as presented by the Theatre Guild
(Photograph by Muray)

Walter Hampden as Cyrano
(Courtesy of The New York *Times*)

True T. Thompson in Philip Barry's   True T. Thompson in *In the Smokies*
You and I

Joseph Urban's design for a setting for *Pelleas and Melisande*

Joseph Urban's design for a setting for *Carmen*

Irving Pichel as Kurano in Masefield's *The Faithful*
(Photograph by Armer)

Jane Cowl (Photograph by Muray)

Walter Hampden and Nazimova in Ibsen's *The Masterbuilder*

Mrs. Fiske as Rebecca West in Ibsen's *Rosmersholm*

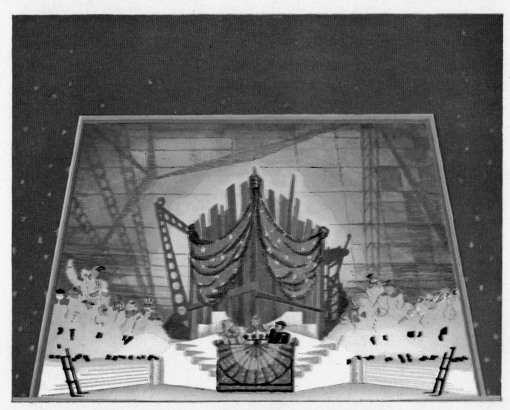

Donald Oenslager's design for a setting for Aristophanes' *The Birds*

Lillian Gaertner's design for a decoration for the Laboratory Theatre, New York

Another Gaertner design for the Laboratory Theatre

Egon Brecher and Eva Le Gallienne in Chekov's *The Three Sisters*

A scene from Hampden's production of *Cyrano de Bergerac*
(Scenic design by Claude Bragdon)

Scene designed by Nicholas Remisoff for Offenbach's *The
Little Circus*

The Neighborhood Playhouse presentation of *The White Peacock* (Costumes by
Aline Bernstein; ballet by Irene Lewisohn)

239

An eighteenth-century New Orleans French mansion setting designed by Donald Oenslager for the operetta *The New Moon*

Another Oenslager setting for *The Birds*

The Roxy Theatre, New York

Egyptian Theatre, Hollywood, Cal.

The Theatre Guild Theatre, New York

Interior of the Theatre Guild Theatre

Mordecai Gorelik's design for John Howard Lawson's *Processional*

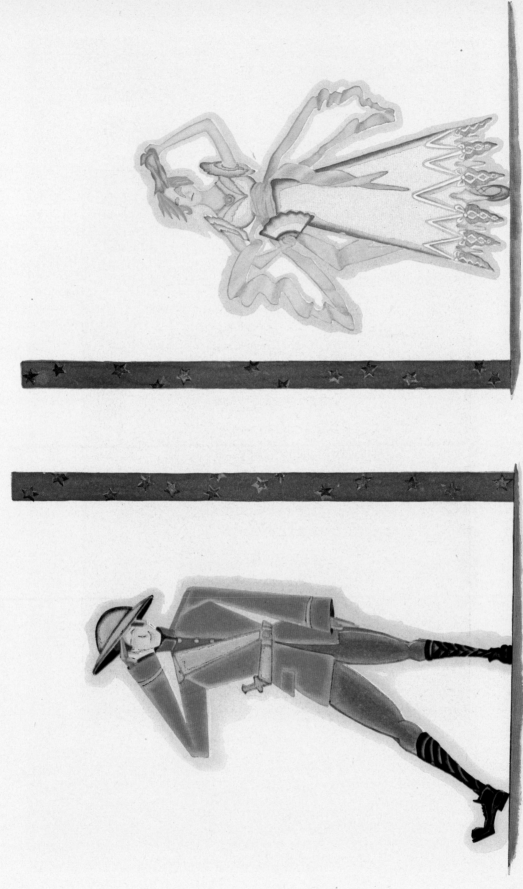

Sketches by Donald Oenslager for Stravinsky's *The History of a Soldier*, produced at the Jolson Theatre in 1928

The foyer of the Theatre Guild Theatre

The Ziegfeld Theatre, New York, designed by Joseph Urban

Robert Edmond Jones' sketch for *The Skyscraper Ballet*

248

Sketch by Mordecai Gorelik for Michael Gold's *Fiesta*

Another sketch by Gorelik for *Fiesta*

Joseph Urban's design for the main façade of an opera house

Another Urban design for an opera house

Norman-Bel Geddes' "Comic Supplement" sketch

Sketch for costume design of slave by Lee Simonson

Another view of Urban's design for an opera house

A gigantic and monumental Urban design for an opera house

An Urban sketch for the proscenium of an opera house

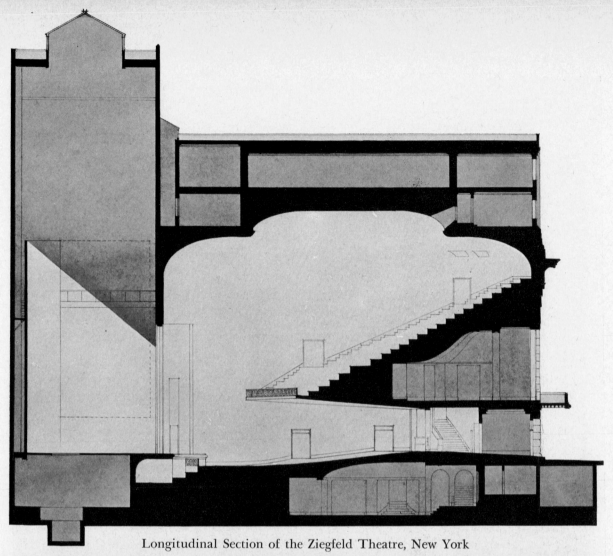

Longitudinal Section of the Ziegfeld Theatre, New York

Sketch for lobby of theatre by Joseph Urban

257

Scene from Paul Sifton's *The Belt* as presented by the Cherry Lane Players

Cleon Throckmorton's setting for O'Neill's *All God's Chillun Got Wings,* as presented at the Provincetown Playhouse

Sketch by Boris Anisfeld for *Love of
Three Oranges*

Reginald Marsh's curtain design for Melchior Lengyel's *Sancho Panza*

Jo Mielziner's design for *Faust*

Mielziner's design for O'Neill's *Strange Interlude*

270

Sketch for costume design of Solomon's bodyguard
by Lee Simonson

Raymond Johnson's design for *Medea*

Manuel Essman's design for the epilogue of a *Human Allegory*

Mordecai Gorelik's design for Andreyeff's *King Hunger*

Gorelik's design for another scene from *King Hunger*

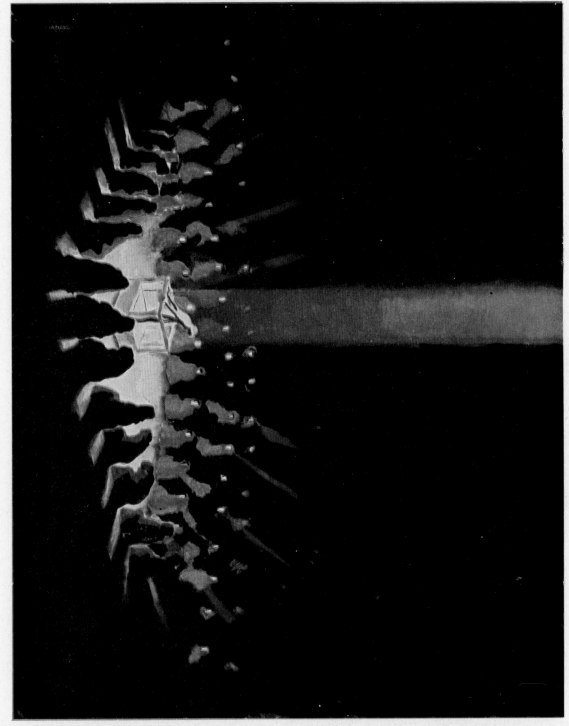

Sketch by Norman-Bel Geddes for *Joan of Arc*

Sketch by Norman-Bel Geddes for *The Divine Comedy*

Gorelik's design for John Howard Lawson's *Processional*

Lee Simonson's design for George Bernard Shaw's *Back to Methusalem*

Mordecai Gorelik'

Fourth of July

A Simonson design for O'Neill's *Dynamo*

Simonson's design for Ernst Toller's *Masse Mensch*

Simonson's design for *Overtones*

Another sketch by Norman-Bel Geddes for *The Divine Comedy.*

Sketch by W. C. Menzie's for oriental street scene for the motion picture, *The Son of the Sheik*

Simonson's design for another scene from *Masse Mensch*

Simonson's design for Tolstoy's *Powers of Darkness*

Simonson's design for Faust's study

Simonson's design for the cathedral scene from *Faust*

Sketch by W. C. Menzies of setting for a dungeon chamber scene for a motion picture

Simonson's design for Ibsen's *Peer Gynt*

Simonson's design for the death scene in *Faust*

Simonson's design for a scene for *Marco Millions* by Eugene O'Neill

Another Simonson-designed scene for *Marco Millions*

Simonson's design for a scene in *As You Like It*

Simonson's design for another scene in *As You Like It*

Scene designed by Simonson for *The Faithful*

Scene from *Back to Methusalem,* designed by Simonson

Robert Edmond Jones (Photograph by Edward R. Dickson)

Robert Edmond Jones' design for a scene from *Macbeth*

Another Jones-designed scene for *Macbeth*

A Jones-designed setting for John Barrymore's production of *Richard III*

Photograph by Ralph Steiner of New York street, showing his influence on scenic designing

Cleon Throckmorton's setting for the New York bridge scene in *Adam Solitaire,* as presented at the Provincetown Playhouse

Herman Rosse's design for Gershwin's *Rhapsody in Blue*

Another setting designed by Rosse for Gershwin's *Rhapsody in Blue*

Rosse's setting for *A South Sea Island Fantasy*

Rosse's setting for *A Revue in a Nutshell*

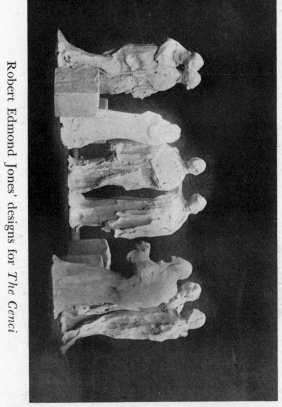

Robert Edmond Jones' designs for *The Cenci*

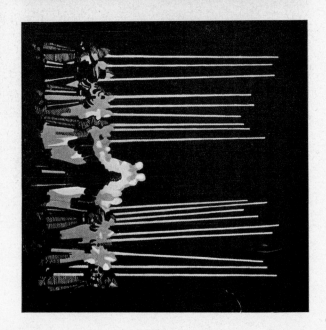

Jones' design for *Faust*

Jones' design for *La Gioconda*

Strindberg's *Ghost Sonata,* as presented by the Provincetown Players, under the direction of Robert Edmond Jones and James Light

Jones-designed mask for the character "Caliban"

Helen Gahagen in a Jones-designed setting for Provincetown Playhouse production of *Beyond*

Jones' setting for Pirandello's *Living Mask*

Jones' setting for *Serena Blandish*

Norman-Bel Geddes
(Photograph by Francis Bruguière)

Norman-Bel Geddes' setting for *Joan of Arc*

Norman-Bel Geddes' setting for another scene for *Joan of Arc*

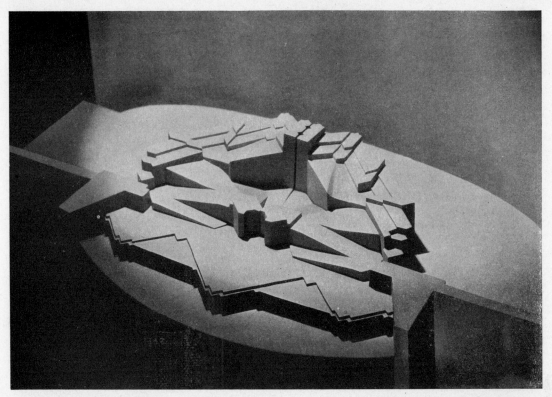

Norman-Bel Geddes' model for permanent setting for O'Neill's *Lazarus Laughed*

Another view of Norman-Bel Geddes' model for setting for *Lazarus Laughed*

Norman-Bel Geddes' design for *King Lear* setting

Another Norman-Bel Geddes design for a setting for *King Lear*

Another scene designed by Norman-Bel Geddes for *King Lear*

Norman-Bel Geddes' design for the cathedral for Max Reinhardt's production of *The Miracle* (Century Theatre, New York, 1924)

Sketch of Norman-Bel Geddes' setting for *The Miracle*

Setting from *The Miracle,* showing how orchestra was converted into interior of cathedral

Figures designed by Norman-Bel Geddes for *The Miracle*

Norman-Bel Geddes' project for *The Divine Comedy*

Frank Conroy, Dudley Digges and Peter
Holden in *On Borrowed Time*
(Photograph by Lucas & Pritchard)

Henry Travers as "Gramps" in
You Can't Take It With You
(Photograph by Vandamm)

Frank Craven, Martha Scott and John Craven in Thornton Wilder's *Our Town*
(Photograph by Vandamm)

Scene from the Mercury Theatre's production of *Julius Caesar,* directed by Orson Welles
(Photograph by Lucas & Pritchard)

Lynn Fontanne and Alfred Lunt in Robert E. Sherwood's *Idiot's Delight*
(Photograph by Vandamm)

PHOTOGRAPHIC SECTION

THE MOTION PICTURE IN AMERICA

Dramatic pictorial effect through the use of perspective and light contrast. Scene sketched by W. C. Menzies shows escaping prisoners caught by the spotlights

Sketch by A. Grot of a courtyard in Moscow, to be used in designing cinema set for a film

Sketch by W. C. Menzies of a prison break, showing how cinema technique
develops new sight angles

Sketch by A. Grot of the gangway to a ship's hold, showing how new sight angles are
developed by the cinema

Sketch by A. Grot showing how the cinema heightens dramatic effect by using
unusual perspective

A sketch by A. Grot of a stage, showing how motion picture technique introduces
new sight angles

Film technique light effect, as sketched by Usher

Sketch for entrance to royal castle, by Usher and Menzies, for the picture
Madame Dubarry. Perspective is here used as a means of expression

View from dirigible gondola of landing crew, showing how film technicians
find original picture motifs

Sketch for angles to be later employed in shooting picture. This shows a
landing crew mooring a dirigible

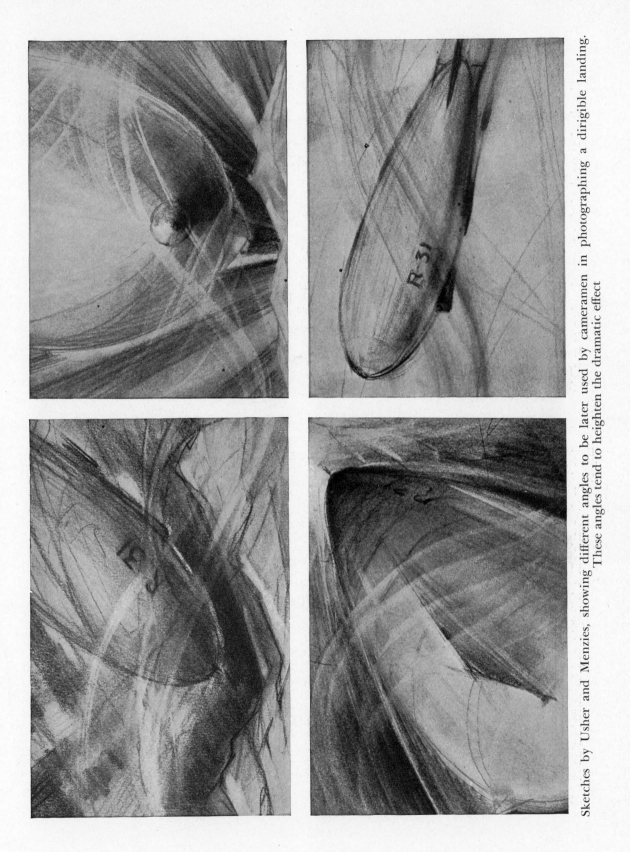

Sketches by Usher and Menzies, showing different angles to be later used by cameramen in photographing a dirigible landing. These angles tend to heighten the dramatic effect

Sketch of scene depicting a man leaping over a chasm, showing how dramatic effect is heightened by introduction of new visual angles

Sketch by Usher showing sequence of shots of burglary scene for the picture *Raffles*

Here Ohmann and Menzies introduce new visual angles in a scene showing the
entrance to the White House, for the picture *Abraham Lincoln*

Sketch by Ohmann and Menzies for dramatic night scene inside White House, for the
picture *Abraham Lincoln*

Sketch by Ohmann and Menzies for garden-party scene in *Madame Dubarry*

Perspective and lighting emphasize the luxuriousness of Madame Dubarry's boudoir in this scene from *Madame Dubarry*

Unusual perspective of man climbing wall of house. Dramatic effect is considerably heightened by the angle employed

Sketch by Usher for a harrowing scene for a mystery picture

Rembrandtesque light effect employed by Usher and Menzies in the picture
Abraham Lincoln

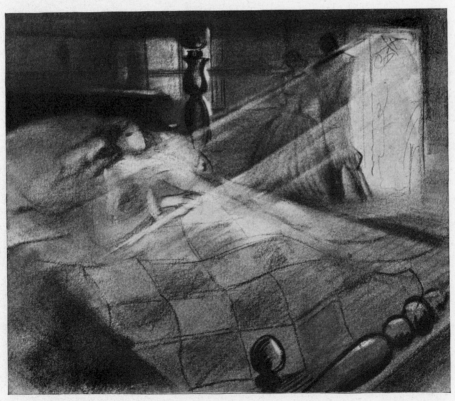

Another painting effect employed by the cinema. This is also a scene from
Abraham Lincoln

Sketch for the beggars' den scene in the film *The Vagabond King* (W. C. Menzies)

Phantasmagorical scene sketched by A. Gruenberger for *Atlantis*

Another sketch by Gruenberger for *Atlantis*

Sketch by Grot designed to emphasize the "aloneness" of a ship at sea

Sketch by A. Grot for a fairyland scene in *The Thief of Bagdad*

Sketch by Menzies for a scene for the Fairbanks-Pickford production of
The Taming of The Shrew

Sketch by Usher of the "Through the Looking Glass" scene for
Alice in Wonderland

Sketch by A. Grot for *The King of Kings*. This scene of Christ before the people is a good illustration of pictorial composition in the motion picture

Gallows scene by A. Grot, showing how painting effects are approximated

Sketch by Gruenberger for setting to represent the bedroom of a Russian princess

Sketch by Gruenberger of setting for the picture *The Volga Boatman*

A painting-like quality is here attained by A. Grot in a sketch for a setting of a country doctor's waiting-room

Sketch for dramatic scene of a doctor's night call

Sketch of room in a country house for the picture *The Comedy of Life*

Sketch by A. Grot for the rooftops setting in *The Falcon's Nest*

Sketch for an Algiers street-scene setting by A. Grot

Venetian street-scene setting by A. Grot for the film *The Comedy of Life*

Sketch by A. Grot of the road to Siberia for a film setting

Sketch for a setting of a circus in a factory town

Sketch for the setting of the princess' room for the picture *The Thief of Bagdad*

The princess' room setting as it actually appeared in the picture

Sketch for the scene depicting the departure of the sultan in *The Thief of Bagdad*

Sketch of scene for *The Thief of Bagdad*. This setting has been designed to permit Douglas Fairbanks ample room for his characteristic acrobatics

Sketch showing use of the romantic technique in the motion picture

The romantic technique as employed in showing interior of a machine room

Sketch for an elaborate cabaret setting, designed by Gruenberger

Sketch of interior of boiler room, designed by A. Grot

Sketch showing how expressionistic effect is produced by directed lighting

Sketch for scene showing a prison line-up, by W. C. Menzies

Montage effect designed by W. C. Menzies. This one he calls "Metropolitan Symphony"

Expressionism is here utilized to emphasize the dramatic values of a scene
depicting a religious miracle

Another example of expressionism as an aid to highlight the drama of a scene showing
a religious vision

Modern interior designed by Gibbons. Note the use of surfaces which mirror light in various ways

Modern bar setting designed by Gibbons

Living-room setting in the modern manner, designed by Gibbons

A modern interior for a motion picture

A modern and palatial interior setting, designed by Gibbons

A modern music-room setting by Gibbons

A phantasmagorical setting by Gibbons

Promenade of the Paramount Theatre, New York

The auditorium of the Roxy Theatre, New York

The Paramount Theatre Building, New York

Lobby of the Roxy Theatre, New York

356

Samuel Goldwyn. The lady with the black hat is Geraldine Farrar

One of the first stars: the dancer Annabelle

Two early American film stars.
On the left, Lois Meredith; on the right, Helen Wolcott

William Fox

Adolph Zukor

Jesse L. Lasky

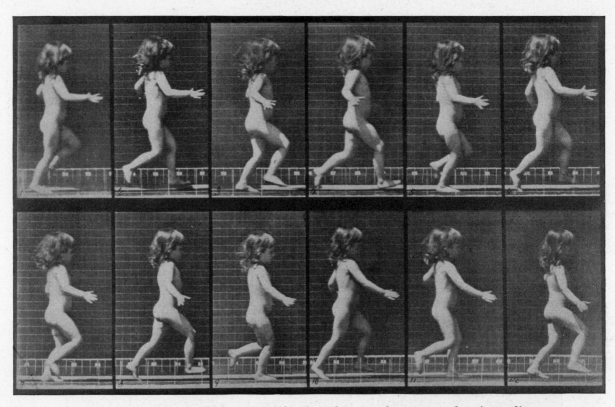

This series of stills by Muybridge, the California photographer, was the immediate precursor of motion pictures

This picture of an outdoor set, from the talking picture *The Floradora Girl,* shows the complicated preparations which must be made

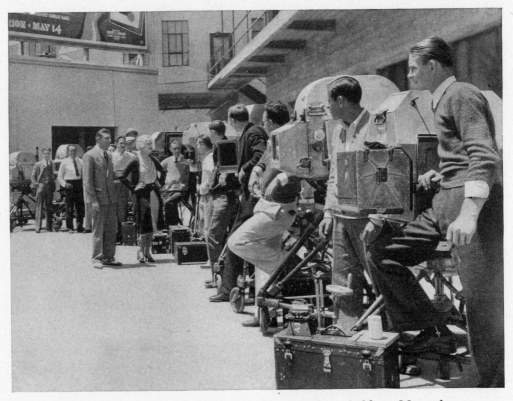

Cameramen with their equipment on the Metro-Goldwyn-Mayer lot

D. W. Griffith, the creator of modern production technique

Hobart Bosworth, a pioneer actor and director

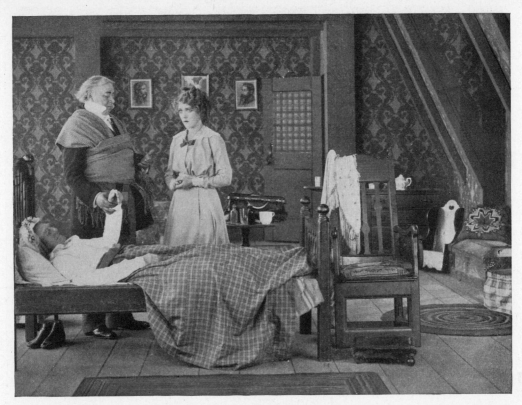

Mary Pickford in one of her first starring rôles. This is a scene from
A Good Little Devil

Sarah Bernhardt in her sole picture, *Elizabeth*. This European production inspired Zukor to make
pictures with "Famous Players"

Mary Pickford in an early picture

Mary Pickford and Douglas Fairbanks welcome the Japanese star Komaka Sunada to Hollywood

An early film showing the exaggerated acting used to denote pathos

A tragic scene from an early picture. Painted props and backdrop were generally used

A typical scene from an early film. Theatre technique was employed in the disposition
of actors on the stage

The sadistic instinct creeps into the early motion picture *Rose of the Rancho*

Theda Bara inaugurates the "vamp" type in *A Fool There Was*

Eroticism begins to influence the early motion picture. Here is the dancer Carmencita in a provocative pose

Mary Pickford in a love scene in an early picture

Norma Shearer in an early picture introduces the modern American girl type to
cinema audiences

The first film studio: Edison's moving picture workshop, called "The Black Maria," in 1900

A 1908 film studio in Los Angeles

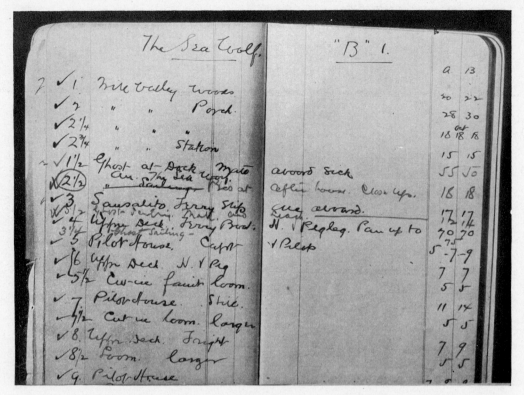

One of the first shooting scripts. This one was used in Hobart Bosworth's production of *The Sea Wolf*

Mary Pickford in a war film, in 1917

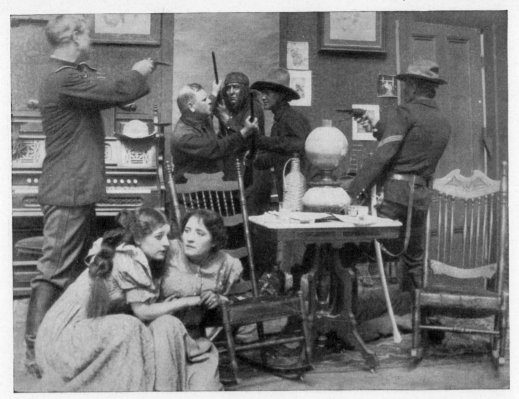

Scene from a typical 1913 Wild West film. All of the action is crowded into a small area

Typical fight scene from a 1915 Wild West picture

One of the exaggerated scenes so common in early Wild West pictures. This one was made in 1915

Scene from a more recent Wild West picture, starring Tom Mix. Note the improved technique

Scene from King Vidor's production, *Billy the Kid*, showing how the exotic element is stressed

Scene from Griffith's *Intolerance*. In this picture Griffith attempted to show human intolerance. The picture was a commercial failure

The bacchanal scene in *Noah's Ark*

Crowd scene in *Noah's Ark*

Valentino was the first of the ardent Latin types. Here is one of his followers

Douglas Fairbanks created the adventurer type. Here he is in *The Black Pirate*

The Indian actor Baluk

The romantic Negro type as portrayed by Daniel Haynes in *Hallelujah!*

376

Colleen Moore had a tremendous vogue in the twenties

Dolores del Rio was one of the first of the Latin-type women stars

377

Mary Pickford in one of the poses that
established her as "America's Sweetheart"

Greta Garbo when she first came to
Hollywood

May Marsh, an early favorite, who starred in
The Birth of a Nation

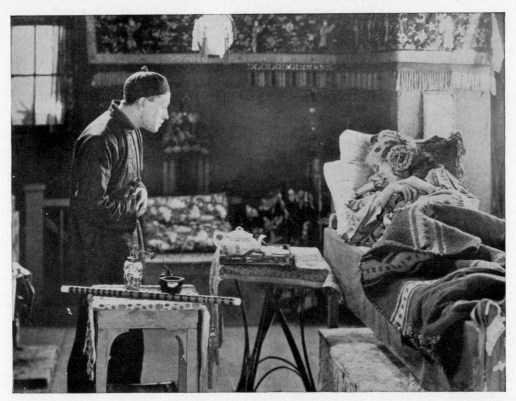

Richard Barthelmess and Lillian Gish in *Broken Blossoms*

Myrna Loy when she still played exotic types. Here she is as an oriental temptress in
The Desert Song

Theda Bara in *Carmen*

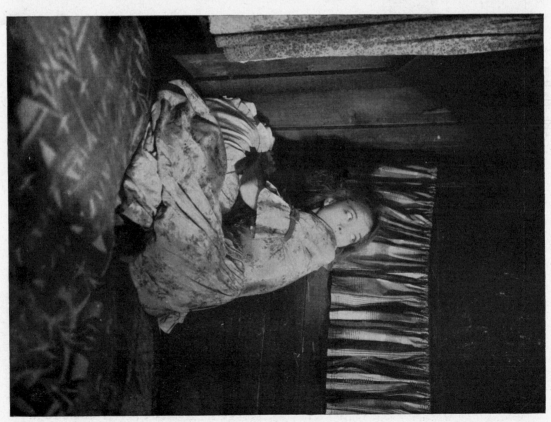

Lillian Gish in one of her typical rôles of a
pathetic, persecuted maiden

Geraldine Farrar in the title rôle of Lasky's production of *Carmen*

Norma Shearer who, more than anyone else, created the picture ideal of the modern American girl

Dolores del Rio in *The Panther*

An example of wish-fulfillment in the motion picture:
Jose Mojica and Mona Mares, in *One Mad Kiss*

The late Lon Chaney, a remarkable character actor, was the creator of the horror type.
Here he is in some typical rôles

Hobart Bosworth in a saloon scene, in 1915

Lon Chaney in *The Unholy Three,* an underworld picture of the twenties

The film director is ever on the alert for new camera angles.
This is a masquerade scene from a revue picture

A "prison girl" scene from a revue picture

Collective eroticism is in evidence in this ballet scene from a musical

Religious ecstasy depicted in a scene from *Hallelujah!*

The wedding scene from *Hallelujah!*

Scene from *The Silent Enemy*, in which native Indians were used

Another scene from *The Silent Enemy*

One of the first Indian films. Bosworth in his rôle in *Atala* (1911)

One of the first close-ups. Hobart Bosworth in a 1910 picture

Hobart Bosworth's 1911 production, *Quo Vadis*

A love scene from *Noah's Ark*

Shots showing how the close-up is employed to emphasize facial expression. The one on the right shows Wallace Beery in *The Big House*

Scene from Josef von Sternberg's celebrated picture, *Underworld*

Mob scenes, like this one from *The Big House,* are handled to perfection

King Vidor, who directed many pictures which marked turning points in film
technique

A great foreign director at work: Jacques Feyder with the company of *Olympia*

Shooting a scene from *La Boheme*. Lillian Gish is Mimi. King Vidor leans on the camera

Shooting a love scene between John Gilbert and Greta Garbo, in *The Green Hat*.
The director is Clarence Brown

Cecil B. De Mille directing a scene for the picture, *Dynamite*

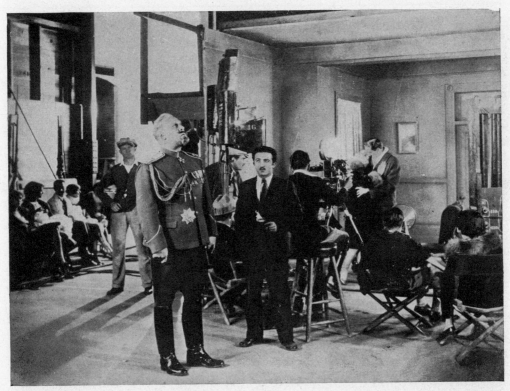

Emil Jannings is being directed by Josef von Sternberg in a scene from *The Last Command*

The escape motif was ever a theme of Douglas Fairbanks' pictures. Here he is in a scene with Anna May Wong in *The Thief of Bagdad*

Luxury for the working girl is the theme of this scene between Joan Crawford and Robert Montgomery

Charlie Chaplin and Ernst Lubitsch

In the foreground are Carl Laemmle and the Russian director Eisenstein

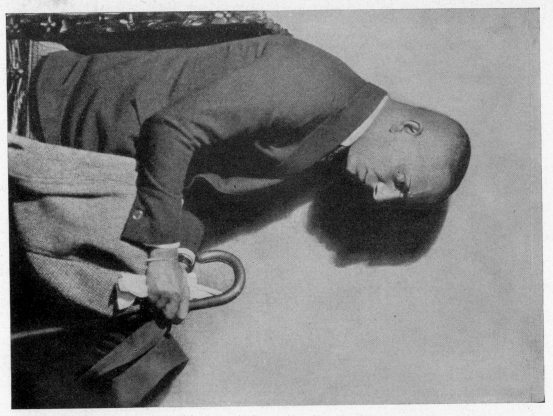

Eric von Stroheim, the famous director

Charlie Chaplin in the developing-room

Harold Lloyd, in character

Mack Sennett

An early American comedy: scene from *A Good Little Devil* (1915)

Mack Sennett (on the extreme right) in one of his early slapstick comedies

A crude comedy scene in *Zaza,* a 1915 film starring Pauline Frederick

The late Will Rogers was the exponent of native and homespun American humor

A typical college comedy scene, from *Good News*

A college dance scene from *Good News*

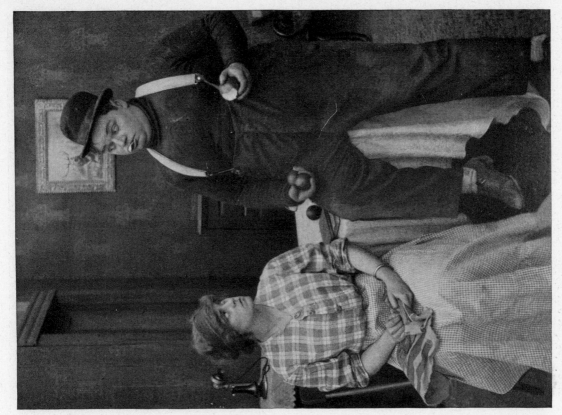

"Fatty" Arbuckle in a comedy scene during his heyday

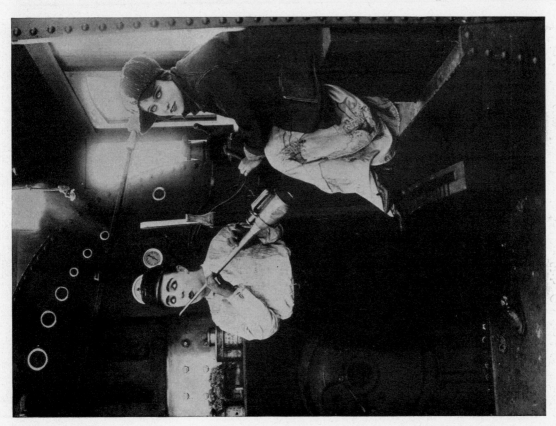

Bobby Vernon and Gloria Swanson in an early Keystone Comedy

Two scenes showing how the producers exploit the public's infantile delight in seeing comedians besmirched by filth. On the left, Chaplin in *The Circus;* on the right, Polly Moran in a comedy scene

The Mack Sennett "Keystone Cops"

Chaplin in an early film. His make-up gradually evolved from the above to its present form

Ben Turpin, whose cross-eyed stare delighted early audiences, about to engage in a pie fight

Chaplin and Turpin in a scene from a Keystone slapstick comedy. Chaplin's make-up has metamorphosed to its present state

406

Present day exponents of the old slapstick technique: Laurel and Hardy

Hardy's heavy-handed *savoir faire* offers the perfect foil for Laurel's lunatic seriousness

Laurel and Hardy in a pie-throwing scene from *The Battle of the Century*

Weber and Fields, in character

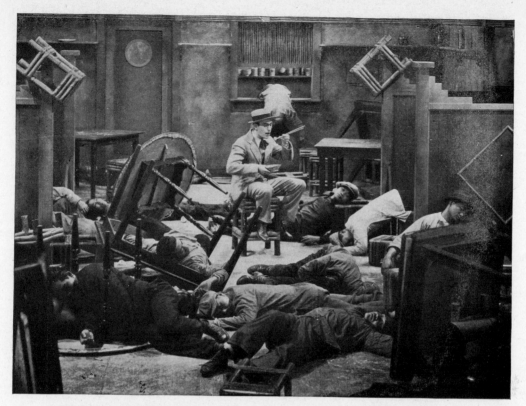

The imperturbable Harold Lloyd in a scene from *Welcome Stranger*

The dead-pan comedian, Buster Keaton, in a scene from *The Camera Man*

Charlie Chaplin, with his eternal enemy, the policeman, in
The Circus

Children comics: The principals of the "Our Gang" series

Animal film: Scene from *Murder in Dog Town*

Charlie Chaplin wearing an early make-up

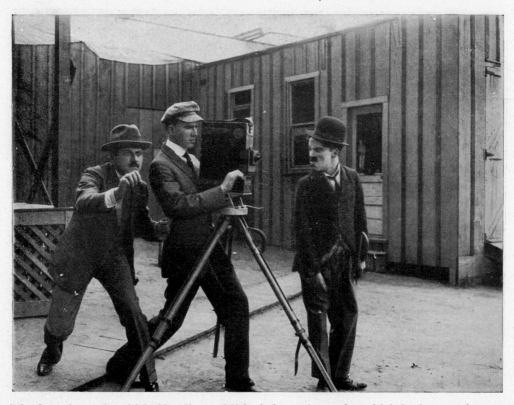

The first picture in which Chaplin established the make-up for which he became famous

Chaplin in an early film with Mabel Normand and Marie Dressler

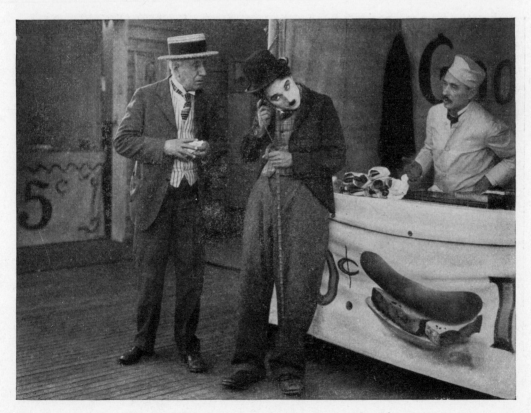

Chaplin and the watch, a scene from *The Circus*

Chaplin as a heckled tightrope walker in *The Circus*

Another typical Chaplin situation: the outsider. This scene is from *The Gold Rush*

A typical humane Chaplin scene from *The Gold Rush*

Here again Chaplin, the puny man with a soul, is vanquished by the man of action:
a scene from *The Gold Rush*

Walt Disney, creator of Mickey Mouse and *Snow White and the Seven Dwarfs*

From left to right: Berthold Viertel, Mrs. Fülöp-Miller, René Fülöp-Miller, Mrs. Schallert and Walt Disney

Svene # 28 (cont-)

----Mickey holding pig so that he
can play on her tits like keys...
while he pushes in and out on her
body like accordion.....Very goofy
exagerated action .....pigs mouth
opens and closes with action of
pumping of body...... When he
finishes he throws her back into
place and the little pigs whish
have been watching and keeping
time, give a dive for her as soon
as she lands and start nurseing
again in time to music....mickey
dances off scene........
SOUND EFFECT of pig accordion
should be a rather discordant
effect......

Scene # 29.

Medium shot of little girl turning
goats tail like crank....and music
of ' Turkey in the Straw ' comes
out his mouth like hand organ....

As she cranks che does crazy clog
dance........

Scene # 30.

C.U. of Mickey drumming on bucket
Old cows head sticking in left side
of scene....she is chowing in time
to music.....she reaches over and
licks Mickeys face with her long
tongue....then smiles (shows teeth)
Mickey sees teeth....opens her mouth
wide and hammers on her teeth like
playing Xylophone....plays in time to
music....runs up and down scale, etc.
   Just as he is about to finish two
large feet(the Captains) walk into
right side of scene and stop....Mickey
finishes piece with 'Ta-da-de-da-...
on cows horns....pulls out her tongue
and strums 'Dum - Dum...' on it...and
turns around to girl with smile....He
sees feet...looks upslowly...when he
sees its Captain he acts surprised...

Part of the scenario of a Mickey Mouse picture

Paul Muni, in the title rôle of *The Life of Louis Pasteur*

Muni, in the title rôle of *The Life of Emile Zola*

The flood scene, in the film *In Old Chicago*

Shirley Temple, in *Just Around the Corner*

Sonja Henie, the skating star, in *My Lucky Star*

Ruby Keeler, in a spectacular scene from the picture *42nd Street*

Alice Faye, in *Alexander's Ragtime Band*

Errol Flynn and Olivia de Havilland, in
Robin Hood

Tyrone Power, in a scene from *Suez*

BIBLIOGRAPHY

A GENTLEMAN RESIDING IN THIS CITY: *The Picture of New York, or The Traveller's Guide Through the Commercial Metropolis of the United States.* I. Riley & Co., New York, 1807.

BRICKER, HERSCHEL L.: *Our Theatre Today.* Samuel French, New York, 1936.

BROWN, JOHN MASON: *The Modern Theatre in Revolt.* W. W. Morton & Co., New York, 1929.

BROWN, JOHN MASON: *Upstage, The American Theatre in Performance.* W. W. Norton & Co., New York, 1930.

BROWN, T. A.: *A History of the New York Stage.* 3 vols. 1903.

CLARK, BARRETT H.: *An Hour of American Drama.* J. B. Lippincott Company, Philadelphia, 1930.

CLARK, BARRETT H.: *Eugene O'Neill.* Robert M. McBride, New York, 1926.

CRAIG, EDWARD GORDON: *On the Art of the Theatre.* Small, Maynard & Co., Boston, 1924.

CRAWFORD, MARY CAROLINE: *Romance of the American Theatre.* Little, Brown & Co., Boston, 1925.

DALY, JOSEPH FRANCIS: *The Life of Augustin Daly.* New York, 1917.

DEUTSCH, HELEN AND HANAU, STELLA: *The Provincetown.* Farrar and Rinehart, New York, 1931.

DICKINSON, THOMAS H.: *Playwrights of the New American Theatre.* The Macmillan Company, New York, 1925.

EATON, WALTER PRICHARD: *The Actor's Heritage.* Atlantic Monthly Press, Boston, 1924.

EATON, WALTER PRICHARD: *The Theatre Guild, The First Ten Years.* (With articles by the Directors.) Brentano's New York, 1929.

FLANAGAN, HALLIE: *Federal Theatre Plays.* 2 vols. New York, Random House, 1938.

HAMILTON, CLAYTON: *Problems of the Playwright.* 1917.

HAMILTON, CLAYTON: *Studies in Stagecraft.* 1914.

HORNBLOW, ARTHUR: *A History of the Theatre in America.* 2 vols. J. B. Lippincott, Philadelphia, 1919.

MACGOWAN, KENNETH: *Footlights Across America.* Harcourt, Brace & Co., New York, 1929.

BIBLIOGRAPHY

MacGowan, Kenneth: *The Theatre of Tomorrow*. Boni & Liveright, New York, 1921.

MacKaye, Percy: *Epoch, the Life of Steele MacKaye*.

Marcosson, Isaac F. and Frohman, Daniel: *Charles Frohman, Manager and Man*. Harper & Brothers, New York.

Mayorga, Margaret: *A Short History of the American Drama*.

Moses, Montrose J.: *The American Dramatist*. Little Brown & Co., Boston, 1925.

Moses, Montrose J. and Gerson, Virginia: *Clyde Fitch and His Letters*. Little Brown & Co., Boston, 1924.

Moses, Montrose J. (Editor and introduction to each play) : *Representative Plays by American Dramatists*. 3 vols. E. P. Dutton, New York, 1925.

Moses, Montrose J. and Brown, John Mason (Editors): *The American Theatre as Seen by Its Critics, 1752-1934*. W. W. Norton & Co., New York, 1934.

Mowatt, Anna Cora: *Autobiography of an Actress, or Eight Years on the Stage*. Ticknor & Fields, Boston, 1854.

Nathan, George Jean: *Since Ibsen*. Alfred A. Knopf, New York, 1933.

Odell, George C. D.: *Annals of the New York Stage*. 10 vols. to date. Columbia University Press, New York, 1927 to 1938.

Phelps, William Lyon: *Essays on Modern Dramatists*.

Quinn, Arthur Hobson: *A History of the American Drama*. 2 vols. F. S. Crofts & Co., New York, 1937.

Sanborn, Ralph and Clark, Barrett H.: *O'Neill Bibliography*. Random House, New York, 1931.

Towse, John Ranken: *Sixty Years of the Theatre*. Funk & Wagnalls Co., New York.

Whitman, Willson: *Bread and Circuses*. The Oxford Press, New York, 1937.

Winter, William: *The Life of David Belasco*. 2 vols. Moffat, Yard & Company, New York, 1918.

Winter, William: *The Wallet of Time*. 2 vols. Moffat, Yard & Company, New York, 1913.

Young, Stark: *The Flower in Drama*. Charles Scribner's Sons, New York, 1923.

Young, Stark: *The Theatre*. George H. Doran, New York, 1927.

INDEX

INDEX

426

INDEX

INDEX

West, Benjamin, 20
Westley, Helen, 68
What Price Glory, 94
Whitman, Walt, 43
Wignell, 20
Williamsburg, 8, 13
Winter, William, 42
Winterset, 94, 95

Woollcott, Alexander, 79, 93

Ye Bare and Ye Cubb, 8
Yeats, William Butler, 60
Yellow Jack, 96
You Can't Take It With You, 43

ZUKOR, Adolph, 106, 107, 112, 130